STILL

ME, Lucy, AND THE

LORD

DEVOTIONALS TO GUIDE YOU BACK TO THE SIMPLICITY OF WALKING WITH JESUS

DON HOCKER

HIGH BRIDGE BOOKS
HOUSTON

This book is dedicated to all who got a copy of my first book, *Just Me, Lucy, and the Lord*. May God bless you always!

To Lydia

May God's grace + peace Be with You!

Don Hocker

12/14/23

CONTENTS

Introduction 1

Day One: A Recognition From Jesus 5

Day Two: Light Vs. Darkness 9

Day Three: God Is Enough 13

Day Four: Breakfast with Jesus 17

Day Five: Justification 21

Day Six: The Question 25

Day Seven: Adoption 29

Day Eight: Little Children 33

Day Nine: Listening 37

Day Ten: Life's Total Package 41

Day Eleven: The Aroma Of Christ 47

Day Twelve: A Revival 51

Day Thirteen: Encouragement 55

Day Fourteen: To God Be The Glory 59

Day Fifteen: Posterity 63

Day Sixteen: Almost Christian 67

Day Seventeen: Tragedy 71

Day Eighteen: The Rapture 75

Day Nineteen: God Loves The Sinner 79

Day Twenty: No Other Gods 83

Day Twenty One: The Holy Spirit 89

Day Twenty-Two: Giving Thanks 93

Day Twenty-Three: Strength And Courage 97

Day Twenty-Four: The Servant 101

Day Twenty-Five: Patience 105

Day Twenty-Six: The Temporary Life 109

Day Twenty-Seven: The Extraordinary 113

Day Twenty-Eight: The Plan 117

Day Twenty-Nine: God's Protection 121

Day Thirty: Making the Death of Jesus Personal 125

Day Thirty-One: God's Love 129

Conclusion: A Prayer From Jesus 133

INTRODUCTION

BECAUSE OF EACH AND EVERY ONE OF YOU, MY FIRST BOOK, *JUST ME, Lucy, and the Lord,* was a success! No, it is not on the New York Times Bestseller list for 2022. No, not anywhere close. It has been a success because I am convinced that, in my small community of Laurens, South Carolina, and surrounding areas, there is a strong desire for God's word, that people are so kind, and that people are very generous.

From the very beginning, I decided that I would make nothing off the book. I would give the book away to whoever wanted a copy, and if they were so inclined, I explained that they were free to make a donation and that 100% of the donation would go to charity.[1] I started out placing copies of the book in local churches, giving them directly to friends and family, and then I had a book signing at a local coffee shop. The book signing was advertised in the local newspaper and on our local radio station, and fliers were placed in businesses across the county. It was a major success. More than 100 people attended (some of whom I did not know), and many donations were collected.

Before I go any further, I need to say this: All the credit for all the positives coming out of my first book goes to God. He is deserving of all of the credit. Praise God! I am simply thankful that He decided to use me as His tool in getting His Word out. Here is a sampling of some comments made to me by note, email, text, reviews on Amazon, or simply in conversation:

- "Such a great book and very inspiring."
- "It is simple, enjoyable to read."
- "I have read it 3 times and am now memorizing the scripture passages."
- "The book is wonderful. What a gift to the town. Lives will be touched."
- "We are finding your simple understanding of scripture to be just the words we can understand and be inspired by."
- "This little book has everything you need at your fingertips for inspiring daily devotions from beginner to the most experienced disciple of Jesus."
- And my favorite: "I can't wait to read this bad boy!"

You can tell from what some people had to say about *Just Me, Lucy, and the Lord* that it was simple and easy to understand. If you go back to the book's Introduction I stated, "I am not an expert theologian. I am not a bible scholar. … The devotionals simply contain my simple understanding of what the various scripture passages mean to me." No hype there. I was true to my word.

Also in the book's Introduction, I said "If this modest devotional book touches one person in a special way, then I will be forever grateful and truly humbled." I can tell you right now I have truly been humbled beyond measure, and I am forever grateful!

For those of you who have not read my first book, you may be wondering who Lucy is. Well, Lucy was our beloved dachshund who spent many mornings with me during my quiet time with the Lord. She continues to be greatly missed.

Finally, some have asked me over this past year if I was going to write another devotional book. Well, here you go! I hope you enjoy it!

God is good! All the time!

---

[1] So far, the charities I have given to with 100% of donations (and 100% of sale proceeds) have been Samaritan's Purse in Boone, North Carolina; St. Jude Children's Hospital in Memphis, Tennessee; Shriner's Children's Hospital in Greenville, South Carolina; and Harvest Ministries and Greg Laurie in Riverside, California. Some people made donations in my name (and Gayle's, my wife) to their charity of choice.

Day One

A RECOGNITION FROM JESUS

When the members of the Sanhedrin heard this, they were furious and gnashed their teeth at him. But Stephen, full of the Holy Spirit, looked up to heaven and saw the glory of God, and Jesus standing at the right hand of God. "Look," he said, "I see heaven open and the Son of Man standing at the right hand of God." At this they covered their ears and, yelling at the top of their voices, they all rushed at him, dragged him out of the city and began to stone him. Meanwhile, the witnesses laid their coats at the feet of a young man named Saul.

—Acts 7:54-58 NIV

Will you do something for me? Will you go back and read this passage of scripture several more times?

See if anything jumps out at you. Do you need a hint? What about that Jesus was *standing* at the right hand of God? So many times in scripture, Jesus is always referred to as seated or sitting down at the right hand of God.[1] I will talk more about Jesus standing and the implications of this in a moment.

Let's look at what took place with Stephen before he was stoned to death. Stephen was taken into custody by the ruling religious leaders of the day known as the Sanhedrin. In responding to the charges levied against him, Stephen gave these religious leaders a history lesson concerning Abraham and Moses. Then, without any hesitation and with the power of the Holy Spirit at his side, he let these guys have it. As if to pull it out of Jesus' playbook, Stephen called them stiff-necked people, always resisting the Holy Spirit.[2] Then in the next verse, he said "And now you have betrayed and murdered him"—meaning Jesus. Stephen knew what was going to happen. He knew his life was on the line. Stephen was willing to die for his faith. Would we not want to have that kind of faith?

So now let's shift our focus to Jesus. When Jesus was on this earth, He had an earthly mission to preach and teach and to fulfill one part of God's eternal plan to die on the cross for the forgiveness of our sins. When Jesus left planet Earth to be with His Father, He did not wipe His hands clean and say, "I am done now—I am now going to sit back and relax." This is the farthest thing from the truth. No, He took on his next mission, and that is, based upon Romans 8:34b NIV, that he "is at the right hand of God and is also interceding for us." Many liken this role to a defense attorney advocating for us in a court of law. As part of this intercession by Jesus, He is constantly watching us and focusing on us in how we are sharing our faith, how we are living godly lives, and how are we bringing honor and glory to our Father in heaven. My friends, Jesus entered heaven to appear for us in God's presence.[3]

So, why was Jesus standing? Was Jesus honoring Stephen with a standing ovation? I truly believe He was. Wow! Jesus was recognizing and paying tribute to the man of faith that Stephen was and his sacrifice. We know that there is rejoicing in heaven when one repents and comes to faith.[4] Heaven is a place of celebration, and Jesus is always a part of the festivities!

The lesson in all of this is that we should always share and stand up for our faith regardless of the consequences. Fortunately, in this country death is really not an expected consequence, but rejection, scorn, and ridicule are.

We walk the Christian walk not for the applause but because we are commanded to do it and we want to do it. However, the applause and recognition are not bad things. Have you ever been to an event of some kind where either you or a loved one or friend are being recognized for an accomplishment, and when presented with the recognition, there is a standing ovation? What feeling do you have? I always have a tingling sensation with a few extra heartbeats. Would it not be really special if when we do something pleasing to our Jesus, we know that He is standing in applause? Knowing that we have pleased our Savior is a goal that we should always have. We do not work and act for man's applause but for that applause from heaven. It is much more fulfilling and satisfying.

Finally, there is one more observation to make here. As you notice from our passage, the stoning of Stephen was in the presence of Paul (then Saul). Do you think that Stephen's strong stance for his faith had a bigger impact than he would have ever known? Of course, Paul had a tremendous impact on the early church and the Bible. Could it have possibly started with him watching Stephen being stoned? How much bigger a deal is Stephen because of that?

Thought: Do you ever think about Jesus keeping His eye on you? Do you feel His pleasure when you do something for our Father's honor and glory?

Let us pray: Holy Jesus, we pray that all that we do is pleasing to You and brings honor and glory to our Father. Empower us through the power of Your Holy Spirit to share our faith and the good news of the Gospel. Amen.

---

[1] See Ephesians 1:20, Hebrews 1:3, Hebrews 10:12, Hebrews 12:2 (NIV). Note: I checked four other well-known translations, and they all have "standing" so this is not just unique to the NIV translation.

[2] See Acts 7:51 (NIV).

[3] See Hebrews 9:24b (NIV).

[4] See Luke 15:7 (NIV).

Day Two

LIGHT VS. DARKNESS

When Jesus spoke again to the people, he said "I am the light of the world. Whoever follows me will never walk in darkness, but will have the light of life."

—John 8:12 NIV

IS DARKNESS BAD? I THINK IT DEPENDS. CERTAINLY, A LITTLE DARKNESS while watching a good movie on television, providing a cozy and comfortable feeling, is a good thing. And too, I think most people want it fairly dark when sleeping at night.

Darkness can be a bad thing, especially when it causes some anxiety and fear. For example, my office and reception area do not have windows. One afternoon when I was there by myself, the power went off in the entire building, and I was in the bathroom. To make matters worse, I did not have my cell phone with me, so I had no flashlight. I literally could not see my hand in front of my face. So using my familiarity with the layout of my office and the location of office furniture, I slowly and methodically groped my way along, feeling for and touching everything I could to eventually make it to the door. Freedom at last! What a sight it was!

The second example involves the local Boy Scout troop my son, Michael,[1] was very involved in. During trips, I served as a parent volunteer simply because I wanted to be with my son. On one trip, we took the troop to Sweetwater, Tennessee where the world's second-largest underground lake is located. It is called The Lost Sea, and it is in a large 140-foot-underground cavern system. We went exploring throughout the entire area, including crawling through narrow cave tunnels.[2] Granted we had the benefit of flashlights to guide us during our exploration, but at nights, we slept in tents in the cave. When all of the flashlights were turned off, I was back in my office without power. To make matters worse, there were creatures in the cave known as cave rats, and without illumination, sleep was not something easy to come by. I was completely blind in my situations of darkness.

Spiritual darkness—or as some say, spiritual blindness—is not a good thing. There is no joy or purpose. When you are spiritually blind, you just aimlessly go through life grasping for whatever gives some temporary sense of satisfaction or pleasure. Just like me in my office, groping around trying to find the door and the way out. If only I had a flashlight, my way would have been lit, and the predicament would have been easy. The Apostle Paul calls it "fruitless deeds of darkness."[3] Nothing is produced. One who is spiritually blind amounts to a lifeless form of existence without any source of strength. With no ability to see, this person has nothing to guide them through life's troubles. The darkness provides no sense of comfort or peace—just a fear of what lies ahead like the fear of those cave rats.

On the other hand, Jesus is the "light of life," and He promises us light if we follow Him, as we read in our passage for today. If we have Jesus in all that we do, we will have, as Paul says in the Ephesians passage, goodness fruit, righteousness fruit, and truth fruit (paraphrased). We will always have the light—Jesus' light. Jesus always wants us to follow Him. This means that He wants us to walk with Him every day in all that we do. It can also mean, however, as Jesus says, He "will lead the way." So picture this: You are walking with Jesus, and trouble lies ahead. Jesus takes control, and with His flashlight in hand, He points to that temptation and says, "Stay clear." He then points with His flashlight to that trial and says, "Stay close to me, and I will get you through it." He then, again with His trusty flashlight, points to something amazing in your life, and He says, "That shows how much I love you, my child."

We do not want to grope around and stumble in darkness. No, we want Jesus' light. The light of His strength, His grace, and His love.

Thought: Do you have the light of Jesus in your life? If not, then invite His light in.

Let us pray: Dear Jesus, we are so grateful that we have Your light of life in every day of our lives to guide and lead us as we follow You. Amen

---

[1] In *Just Me, Lucy, and the Lord*, I referred to my children as Mike and Kathryn, and I am not sure why I did because that is not what I call them. While those are their names they use, I call them Michael and Kat. So in this book, it is Michael and Kat. Fair enough kids?

[2] Now, if one has any amount of claustrophobia, then tunnel crawling should not be on the agenda. Was not on my agenda, for sure!

[3] Ephesians 5:8-11 NIV

Day Three

GOD IS ENOUGH

Because of the Lord's great love we are not consumed, for his compassions never fail. They are new every morning; great is your faithfulness. I say to myself, "The Lord is my portion; therefore I will wait for him."

—Lamentations 3:22-24 NIV

THERE ARE MANY UNCERTAINTIES IN LIFE, BUT THERE ARE THINGS WE DO know with certainty. Here is a short list:

- The sun will rise each morning and set each evening.
- Gravity will keep us firmly planted on the ground.
- Oxygen in the air is what we breathe and what keeps us alive.

- Death, for absolutely everyone, is a certainty, but of course, what is uncertain is when.

- Taxes are a certainty, and we know that Uncle Sam, every April, sticks out his hand for money.

- The sad eyes of my daughter and a quiver of her lip will melt my heart each and every time.[1]

What is also certain is God's love and compassion that He has for us and that He is always faithful. Today, I want to focus on the three major themes in today's passage:

1. God's love keeps us from being consumed.
2. God's compassion for us is new every day.
3. God simply provides.

God's love keeps us from being consumed.

People find it so hard at times to admit and recognize that they are a sinful people. Everyone is born in sin, and sin remains with us until death. To think otherwise is a really risky position to take. God has every right to punish us for our sins, and oftentimes He does to get our attention and bring us to a point of confession, repentance, and change. Every Christian knows that probably the most recognized passage in scripture is John 3:16, and I will paraphrase here—God's love for us was so great that He sent Jesus to this earth so we would not perish but have eternal life. He put His Son, Jesus, on the cross to die so our sins could be forgiven. Otherwise, we would perish. Otherwise, we would be consumed by sin. It is absolutely amazing that God's love for His children is so great, and it is greater than anything one can imagine.

God's compassion for us is new every day.

What exactly is compassion? I looked up the definition of compassion, and this is what a dictionary said: "the feeling that arises when you are confronted with another's suffering and feel motivated to relieve that suffering."

Look at how many times Jesus healed the lame, the deaf, the blind, the demon-possessed, and the dead. Why did He do it? Because He had compassion and mercy for those people. To go one step further, to be truly compassionate, I believe you first must feel empathy. You must feel the emotions and hurt of the other person. Probably one of the best examples of this is the story of Jesus bringing back His good friend, Lazarus, from the dead. When Jesus saw the sisters weeping, He wept as well. He had empathy for the sisters and Lazarus himself. Then Jesus showed His compassion and raised Lazarus from the dead.[2]

God is so compassionate. When today's passage says His compassion is new every day, that means His compassion for us will never stop. There will be a daily dose of it to heal our wounds, ease our worries, and bring us back to His loving arms when we have strayed.

God simply provides.

I love the above phrase which is also quoted in the Book of Psalms: "The Lord is my portion."[3] God provides for our every need, and when He does, whether we admit this or not, it is absolutely enough in the right amount. No more, no less. We humans so often are dissatisfied with what we have, and we have that innate desire for more. But if we would just step back and ponder on the truly many blessings we have, and do this on a regular basis, we will then realize—yes, my plate is full, and it is by the grace of our Heavenly Father that my plate is full. The Apostle Paul reminds us that God will meet all of our needs according to the riches of His glory that we find in our Savior, Jesus Christ.[4]

Let me share with you a quote a friend of mine shared with me several years ago: "Lord, I crawled across the barrenness to you with my empty cup. If only I had known you better, Lord, I would have come running with a bucket."[5] So if we truly know, with certainty, that God is not just going to fill up our cup but our bucket, then, with a grateful heart, we will be satisfied with what God has given us. Let's get our buckets out, shall we!

Thought: What are you certain about God? Are you certain about His love, His compassion, and His provision?

Let us pray: Dear Heavenly Father, please help us when we become dissatisfied with what we have and further help us to know and believe that You, Lord, are our portion. When we doubt Your love and compassion for us, remind us that You love us and will take care of us today and every day of our lives. Amen.

---

[1] When my daughter, Kat, was growing up, she would give me that look—oh, man! I turned to putty!

[2] See John 11.

[3] Psalm 119:57 ESV

[4] See Philippians 4:19 (NIV, paraphrased).

[5] Nancy Spiegelberg is the author of the quote (not the friend).

Day Four

BREAKFAST
WITH JESUS

Jesus said to them, "Bring some of the fish you have just caught." So Simon Peter climbed back into the boat and dragged the net ashore. It was full of large fish, 153, but even with so many the net was not torn. Jesus said to them, "Come and have breakfast." None of the disciples dared ask him, "Who are you?" They knew it was the Lord.

—John 21:10-12 NIV

EXPERTS SAY THAT BREAKFAST IS THE MOST IMPORTANT MEAL OF THE day. I would tend to agree with that. I am a breakfast kinda' guy. I have to have breakfast before I start out on my day. It is really a meal that I cannot skip.[1]

In today's passage, we read that Peter and some of the other disciples had breakfast with Jesus. Breakfast and Jesus. That is a good combination! John gives an account of the third sighting of Jesus after his resurrection. The disciples decide to go fishing, and once again, they are having trouble catching any fish. So when Jesus, the ultimate fisherman, told them to throw their net over the right side of the boat, well, you know the rest of the story. They caught a bunch of fish. What is so neat about this story is that Jesus had been on the shore of the Sea of Galilee that morning, cooking a breakfast of fish and bread over hot coals. When they get to the shore after realizing the man on the shore was, in fact, their Jesus, an invitation is made by Jesus. "Come and have breakfast." Jesus showed up when the disciples least expected Him to, and being the gracious host that He is, Jesus invited them to come.

When you think about it, Jesus offers us invitations all the time, and with every invitation, there is a promise attached. Here are some.

Come, come, and partake of My promise of life to the full.[2] Jesus says that if we have Him in our lives, we will have life to the full. We will be protected, our hearts will not be troubled, and we will have Jesus' company to enjoy every day.

Come, come, and partake of My promise of acceptance.[3] Jesus is telling us that if we are on His team, we are on it for life. We do not have to work or strive to be accepted and loved. Our Father has already chosen us.

Come, come, and partake of My promise of blessings and rewards.[4] Jesus reminds us that whoever accepts the Gospel, much will be given in this age and in the age to come. Just think—when you accepted Christ as Lord and Savior, so many blessings started coming your way, did they not? And the great thing too when difficulties come our way is that Jesus will bless us with strength, bless us with peace, and bless us with comfort.

Let's take this one step further. Every believer after death will come before the Judgment Seat of Christ for a determination on how well we have lived our lives and served God and our brothers and sisters. We will be rewarded accordingly. Now we know that heaven is going to really be a great place, but with rewards, it will even be so much better. It is like icing on the cake. The cake is good, but the icing makes it so much better.

Come, come, and partake of My promise of friendship. [5] Jesus told His disciples the night He was arrested that He now considered them His friends. He offers His friendship to us. We know that Jesus is compassionate, loyal, brave, humble, honest, protective, encouraging, dependable, faithful, forgiving, sacrificial, and loving. Imagine your best friend, Jesus is even better than your best friend. Jesus is a friend that never leaves us. Who would not want a friend in Jesus?

Come, come, and partake of My promise of eternal life. [6] I have said many times that I find it hard to understand that some non-believers think that when you die, that is it. We just cease to exist. Nothing from the last breath to forever. We have a mighty God who created this planet Earth and every single thing on it. He sent His Son, Jesus, to the cross so that our sins would be forgiven. He brought His Son, Jesus, back to life three days later so we can experience the same resurrection as Jesus. You mean to tell me that God simply closes the book when we die and says something like, "It has been nice knowing you. Goodbye!" Absolutely not! We are given the choice, and the two options are heaven and hell. If we choose Jesus, then there is certainly a wonderful life after death.

Throughout scripture, great banquets and feasts are discussed as being a part of heaven. There will be so much celebration in heaven, and I bet a good ole' breakfast will be a part of it. When we reach heaven's gate, I do not believe Peter will be standing there but will certainly be close around. Our Savior Jesus will most certainly be standing there and how wonderful it will be to hear Jesus say, "Come in and enjoy a great breakfast feast that has been prepared for you." And that is a promise I intend to cash in!

Thought: What promises from Jesus have you accepted?

Let us pray: Lord, through Your Son, Jesus Christ, we have been promised so many things. Open our hearts and minds to fully partake of these promises all to Your honor and glory. Amen

---

[1] Oh, man! That sausage and egg casserole that Gayle makes for breakfast! Nothing better!

[2] See John 10:10.

[3] See John 6:37.

[4] See Matthew 5:12.

[5] See John 15:14-15.

[6] See John 10:27-28.

Day Five

JUSTIFICATION

For all have sinned and fall short of the glory of God, and all are justified freely by his grace through the redemption that came by Christ Jesus.

—Romans 3:23-24 NIV

Pretend for a moment that Mastercard, Visa, and American Express all announce that there is no more debt on your credit card, either existing debt or future debt. It has all been done away with, no payment due,[1] no interest due. That is some wishful thinking!

We know that this will never happen with these credit card companies, but it does happen with God's divine credit card. When we sin, we owe a debt, and boy, do we have a lot of debt because we have a lot of sin. God has wiped away every debt and every sin that we have or will have simply because of Christ's death on the cross.

The great thing I like so much about today's passage is that it is so succinct, so concise, and so clearly sets out what the Gospel is all about. It is actually the heart of the Gospel. So let's break down this passage.

Paul talks a lot about justification by faith in his letters to the early churches and to some of his friends. The act of justification is God's declaration that someone is righteous and morally right. So to be justified by faith, the starting point is the absolute realization that I am and you are very sinful people. We are born in sin and continue to sin until we die. Many people do not subscribe to this notion of sin. "I am a good person. I haven't killed anyone or robbed a bank. I think I am good enough to get into heaven." My friends, that attitude will absolutely not get you into heaven but unfortunately will send you straight to hell! Works have never been the answer to salvation. The first sin was the "fruit sin" by Adam and Eve, and sin has continued for everyone throughout history and into the future until Christ returns. It is as simple as that. Realizing that we humans are so far from God's perfection and standard is a great starting point towards salvation.

Secondly, to be justified by faith is to accept God's grace for us, the unmerited favor that God showers on us. It is by God's grace that He used His Son's death to forgive our sins. God hates sin but loves us very much. Nothing more, nothing less.

Thirdly, Jesus' redemptive work on the cross is the culmination of God's grace, His love for us, and His hatred for sin. It has been God's plan all along to help us to strive towards perfection—without sin. He wants us to be as close to the perfect Jesus as we possibly can. He certainly knows, and we should certainly know, that perfection is never attainable by us, but certainly, the journey towards perfection is within our reach.

Lastly, our faith in the cross is vital to this whole process of justification. We must have faith in God's promise that Jesus died on the cross so that our sins will be forgiven. We must know in our heart of hearts that without the cross we are doomed. However, we must recognize that while our faith is important to justification, the ultimate cause is the redemption of Jesus on the cross. Paul said it so well in another letter: "He forgave us all our sins, having canceled the charge of our legal indebtedness which stood against us and condemned us; he has taken it away, nailing it to the cross."[2]

When we accept Jesus as our Lord and Savior, we are coming to God with our sins, our life, and our moral debt. There is no way to pay our debt—we are at our limit. But through Christ's death, if we surrender ourselves to God, He will wipe our slate clean, and we will be united with Jesus in this kingdom and in the kingdom to come.

Thought: How often do you truly believe that you are very sinful and that the only way for your sins to be forgiven is through Jesus Christ on the cross?

Let us pray: Heavenly Father, it is by Your loving grace that we are saved. Our faith allows us to accept the fact that You sacrificed Your Son on the cross so that we could live. Thank you so much, Lord. Amen.

---

[1] Now Gayle, when her credit card bill comes in, she pays the bill before the postal courier has left our street!

[2] Colossians 2:13b-14 NIV. I do not know about you, but my cross has to be an extra-large one! Do they come in this size?

Day Six

THE QUESTION

> *Then the man and his wife heard the sound of the Lord God as he was walking in the garden in the cool of the day, and they hid from the Lord God among the trees of the garden. But the Lord God called to the man, "Where are you?"*
>
> —Genesis 3:8-9 NIV

IMAGINE YOU LIVE IN THE PERFECT PLACE WITH PERFECT FOOD. ALL YOUR needs are met. The only thing forbidden to you is the fruit from just one tree. And then…

Adam and Eve had just eaten the forbidden fruit in the garden. They heard God in the garden, and they knew they had done wrong, so they hid. Then God asked the question, "Where are you?" Now God knew exactly which tree Adam and Eve were hiding behind. God did not need any help from the man to find out where the garden miscreants were located. No, God was asking Adam (and Eve) a question that God asks us on a very regular basis. Where are you in your faith? Where are you in your obedience? Where are you in your repentance?

And how do we respond? When God makes these inquiries of us, do we not hide? Hide behind our pride? Hide behind our selfishness? Do we step up to the plate and admit our mistakes, repent, and seek God's forgiveness. Many times we do not. So let's look at what God requires of us and how we should and should not respond.

Our faith in God is the key to our Christian walk as well as knowing that God loves us and wants the best for us. He makes promises that through our faith we know that He keeps. We should accept this without hesitation. We must be careful, however, that we do not become complacent and take these promises for granted. Look at Adam and Eve. God promised and gave them a wonderful life in the beautiful Garden of Eden, and they took this for granted. We should accept God's promises every day as if the promises were brand new to us. We can live by these promises giving us hope and strength.

Along with God's promises come His commands. When we are commanded by God to not do something, then we better be careful not to do it. If God tells us not to eat the fruit from that one tree, then by golly, we better not eat the fruit from that one tree. See what happened to Adam and Eve. They had it made in the garden. No worries or problems. Just a headache-free time in natural luxury. But once that first sin came about, once that juice from that forbidden fruit touched their lips, game over! Sin entered their world! No more paradise!

God was not happy at all. He came down hard on the serpent (which, of course, He should have), and He also came down hard with punishment on both Adam and Eve. When we sin, God is not happy with us either. He is not happy with us because He loves us and knows what is best for us. We receive His punishment in whatever form he desires. See, we have, as people say, "an audience of one—AO1." God sees all. He knows all. So we think we can hide physically, and God will not see us? Or we hide behind our human weaknesses such as pride and selfishness and believe our sin is no big deal to God? I am here to tell you that every sin is a big deal to God, and we need to truly believe that. So when we sin, we need to go to God and seek His forgiveness.

When we do sin, we need to accept responsibility for our actions and not blame others as Adam and Eve did. Adam pointed the finger at Eve, and Eve pointed the finger at the snake. We need to own up to what we have done and repent of our sins. Repentance is a hard thing to do sometimes, and true and sincere repentance is even harder. Go to God on bended knees with a humble and contrite heart and offer our remorse for what we have done. Now, if repentance does not come after every sin in your life, then it is not going to be all doom and gloom. That is where God's wonderful grace comes in. Thank goodness for His grace. Just remember, God wants us to take ownership of our sins, realizing that God hates sin more than we can ever imagine. Once we do this, then our efforts to become more like Jesus will become more productive and rewarding. Go for the fruit—just not the fruit from that one tree!

Thought: Do you ever think how much it saddens God when we sin and fail to keep His commands? If so, what do you do?

Let us pray: Dear Holy God, You are so full of grace and mercy. You lavish us with grace and extend to us much compassion and mercy when we sin. Please forgive us every time we have made You sad. Help us to never hide from You when we sin and to earnestly strive to obey Your commands, knowing that brings delight and honor to You. Amen

Day Seven

ADOPTION

But when the set time had fully come, God sent his Son, born of a woman, born under the law, to redeem those under the law, that we might receive adoption to sonship. Because you are his sons, God sent the Spirit of his Son into our hearts, the Spirit who calls out "Abba Father." So you are no longer a slave, but God's child; and since you are his child, God has made you also an heir.

—Galatians 4:4-7 NIV

My TWO ADULT CHILDREN ARE BOTH ADOPTED. WE GOT EACH OF THEM when they were just a few days old. Those were two very special days! Gayle and I had tried for several years to have children naturally. We went through fertility procedures and tests but just without any luck. Therefore, wanting children very much, we pursued adoption, and boy, have we been blessed with our two children.[1] We thank God for our infertility issues because without them then there would be no Michael and no Kat in our family.

Spending time together as a family has always been important to us. Allow me to reminisce. While we traveled a lot as the kids were growing up, taking trips to places like New York City, Cancun, and the Bahamas, some of my favorite memories come from simpler moments in our hometown. I can remember one winter when power was out in our little town due to ice and snow. We were without power for several days. Thank goodness for a fireplace and a propane camping stove to heat food and make coffee. But what stands out during that time we spent together is Gayle reading adventure books to us as we laid around by the fire.

Also, I remember those many days and nights watching one of our kids play sports. Whether it was Michael playing football or track and field or Kat running track or playing basketball, we were always there, and the child not playing was always with us cheering their sibling on. Truth be known, I believe that these simple times together were in some ways more important than those trips and cruises. Simply spending time together is the key. The result of all this is that my family is extremely loyal to each other. There is not one thing that one would not do for the other. Our love for each other is very strong!

We believers have been adopted by God, and we have the right to be called "children of God." We are given the right to call God "Abba Father." The privilege to have that intimate relationship with our Heavenly Father and to be a part of God's family is a great blessing among many blessings. The heavenly family with God as our Father and our brothers and sisters in Christ is the ultimate family to have. Our Father in heaven is the ultimate father. He loves us, He protects us, He provides for our needs, He is very loyal to us, and He created a plan where His family will one day be in heaven with Him. Our love for God and His love for us is very strong as well!

Growing up in Sunday School, I always saw pictures of Jesus with people around Him, and many times there were just children (and maybe a lamb or two) with Him. With a little bit of imagination, you could make that picture come alive, hearing Jesus tell those children stories of love, hope, and peace. While I doubt there will be any adventure books in heaven to read, won't it be neat to be sitting around Jesus at His feet and hearing Him quote scripture, talk about parables, and reliving those miracles He performed? I also doubt there will be a fire to sit around with Jesus, but He will provide plenty of warmth. A heavenly family simply being together and enjoying each other. We have hope for that do we not?

Thought: Do you ever think about being a part of God's family and the love you feel and the love you show to others? How real is that love to you?

Let us pray: Abba Father, I know that earthly families are a vital part of Your entire plan, and we thank you so much for our families. We know too that our heavenly family is even more vital to Your plan. We thank You too that we get to be a part of God's family and be a child of the most wonderful and amazing God that You are. Amen.

---

[1] Psalm 127:3 says, "Children are a heritage from the Lord, offspring a reward from him" (NIV). That is a great way to think about our children—a reward!

Day Eight

LITTLE CHILDREN

Then people brought little children to Jesus for him to place his hands on them and pray for them. But the disciples rebuked them. Jesus said, "Let the little children come to me, and do not hinder them, for the kingdom of heaven belongs to such as these." When he placed his hands on them, he went on from there.

—Matthew 19:13-15 NIV

THERE WAS A TELEVISION SHOW IN THE 1960S CALLED *KIDS SAY THE Darndest Things*, hosted by Art Linkletter. He would have four or five kids, usually under the age of six, sitting on stools on stage. Mr. Linkletter would go down the line and ask them different questions, and most of the time the responses would be simple, naïve but very funny. Yet oftentimes they would say things loaded with wisdom at such a tender age.

My soon-to-be four-year-old grandson, Ford, certainly has come up with some zingers of his own, and we call them "Ford-isms"! I will share one funny one and then one that creates the basis for this devotion.

- I asked Ford, "Ford, is it hard being a good boy as you are?" Ford looked up at me and said, "Grandpa, it is tricky!"

- Ford asked Gayle, "Lala, where is your daddy?" Gayle responded, "In heaven with Jesus." Ford said, "Did Pop [Gayle's dad] die"? Gayle said, "Yes." Ford said, "So Jesus made him alive?"

It is what Ford said about Jesus, the insight he displayed, that caused me to truly think about what is so very important about the relationship between children and Jesus. Little children and young people were very important to Jesus, and I believe, and I think others believe, that little children are precious. We can see from Jesus' actions that He feels the same way.

In today's passage, Jesus is very clear that we, as parents and even those adults who are around children, have a very strong and important responsibility to our young children to make sure that they know Jesus. Not just teach them the well-known song so they can sing, "Jesus loves me this I know, for the Bible tells me so... ." No, we need to teach them to truly know Jesus, not just know about Him. So, what do we do? Here are some crucial ways to create a relationship between our little children and Jesus. Without hesitation, I say this responsibility lies on parents and grandparents alike:[1]

Make sure they know that Jesus gave His life for them.

Certainly, Jesus' death on the cross and His resurrection is the foundation for our gospel beliefs. Our children need to know this. They need to know that we are sinful people and that God's plan was to save us from our sinful selves. Thus, Jesus died so our sins would be forgiven. But they need to also know the plan did not stop there. Jesus rose from the dead three days later to prove to everyone that death will not have the final say in a believer's life. They need to know that there is heaven where we will spend eternity with Jesus.

Make sure they know that Jesus is always there for them.

Children need to learn that life is not always easy, that life will have its ups and downs, and that many days will feel like more downs than ups. They need to know that when there is a problem, when there is a difficulty, then they need to look to Jesus, and Jesus will get them through the struggle. He will provide peace, comfort, and encouragement. He will provide guidance and direction to pave the way through the problem, making sure that the right path is taken.

Make sure they know how much Jesus loves them.

To piggyback on the above, we need to instill in our children that Jesus died for us and that God sent His Son to the cross for one basic reason—we are loved. God loves us so much that He allowed His only Son to die for us. We need to instill in them that Jesus loves us so much that He willingly went to the cross and died that horrible death. Simply explain to your children that His death was for the forgiveness of all our sins—past, present, and future. What greater love is that?

Make sure they know how much Jesus means to you.

Our children and our grandchildren need to see how much our faith means to us. Young people typically do not "miss a beat." That was so true for mine. In other words, they are so very observant that they know what is going on around them. So they need to see that we are "walking the walk" and not just "talking the talk." They need to see us in God's word daily. They need to see prayer time as a constant in the home. They need to see active involvement in church and with other believers. They need to see Jesus in us, and when they do, Jesus will be more real to them—will be more alive to them.

It is going to be left up to each of us how much and when we discuss these things. All kids are different, and the timing will be up to each one of us. But we all must accept the responsibility, simply because we love our children and grandchildren so very much, of making sure that Jesus is a big part of their lives. What better way to show our love! What better way did God show His love for us than by giving us Jesus. Thank you, Lord!

Thought: Knowing your children and/or grandchildren, how can you best acquaint your young one with Jesus? What do they respond to the most?

Let us pray: Lord, we thank you for Your Son, Jesus Christ, who paid the ultimate price on the cross for the forgiveness of our sins. Sometimes, Lord, it is simply beyond our comprehension that Your love for us is so great that You would sacrifice Your Son for us, and we are so unworthy. Lord, we pray for our children and grandchildren. Help them to know Jesus and to know and feel Your awesome love. Thank you, Lord, for your awesome love and grace. Amen.

---

[1] So far, Michael and Mandy (my daughter-in-law) and Gayle and I are doing a pretty good job of this, but we cannot stop now! The Bible is constantly read to Ford, Jesus is constantly talked about with him, and prayer time is a daily habit with Ford.

Day Nine

LISTENING

*The Lord came and stood there, calling as at the other times,
"Samuel! Samuel!" Then Samuel said, "Speak, for your servant is listening."*

—1 Samuel 3:10 NIV

I AM GOING TO WAGER A BET[1] THAT THE MAJORITY OF GUYS READING THIS
devotional have had their hearing questioned in some form or fash-
ion by a wife or girlfriend. Am I right? And if the truth were known,
the woman was probably correct. We guys often do a lousy job of
listening to our "better halves" for a myriad of reasons.[2] However,
we could extend this truth further and apply it to both men and
women in our failure to listen to God

Before we explore our inability to carefully listen to God, let's
put today's passage of scripture into context. Samuel, as a young
boy, was placed in the care and teaching of the great priest Eli to

train Samuel in the priestly ways. We know that Samuel would later become one of the great prophets in the Bible. As Eli and Samuel were sleeping, the Lord called out to Samuel, and three times Samuel thought it was Eli calling out to him. Verse 7 clearly says the reason Samuel was mistaken was that "Samuel did not yet know the Lord." Eli finally realized that it was the Lord who was calling out to Samuel, and Eli told him to go back and lie down and when the Lord calls out, say "Speak, Lord, for your servant is listening."

Oh, how often do we miss out on what the Lord is telling us? How often do we fail to listen to God because we do not know Him as we should? Because we have not listened, we think God is not concerned with answering our prayers or not concerned with our problems and trials in our lives. Through the psalmist, God tells us to "Be still and know that I am God."[3] God is telling us, "Stop, be in awe of My presence, and know that I am always concerned with your prayers." God wants us to revere His name and listen to what He has to say. God simply wants us to know Him better.

Now, there are obstacles that get in our way that prevent us from listening to God, and I believe the number one obstacle is the busyness in our lives. We allow the demands of our world around us to cause us not to truly stop and listen, not to stop and soak in His loving presence and guidance.

I have to admit that I often do a poor job of stopping and listening to God. So this devotional is directed at me as much as it is directed at you. I believe that I have a solution that I am going to try, and maybe you can try it too (assuming you have a listening problem too). We all pray. Some pray more than others. So let's try this. First, pray that God will help us know Him better and better each and every day so we will not be like young Samuel. Secondly, before the word "Amen" leaves our mouths, let's keep our eyes closed, keep the noise out of the room and the busy clutter out of our minds, and with a clear head, just listen. With a focus on the awesomeness of God, be attentive to what God has to say. Even though it is certainly possible and within the realm of what God can do, chances are it will not be clearly audible with a voice coming from heaven. No, I believe it will more likely be that tug on the heart—that thought in the head—that feeling of contentment with certainty, knowing God is in control.

Can we stop and not allow our lives' busyness prevent us from daily knowing God better? Can we give God a few minutes out of each day to listen to Him? Can we tune out the clutter that this world hangs around us to listen to our most wonderful and loving God? Can we open up our minds and hearts to receive the bounty of God's goodness? Let's be still and listen, shall we?

Thought: Is busyness the major impediment to stopping and quietly listening to God? Does it prevent you from truly knowing God better? What obstacles are in your way?

Let us pray. Dear Lord, keep us keenly aware of how awesome You are and that there is so much You have for us. Help us to know You better each day and, as we do, to stop and try to listen to You. Oh, there is so much You can tell us. Help us to seek You and always be hungry for Your grace. Amen.

---

[1] I know, I know. I should not be talking about gambling in a Christian devotional book!

[2] "Honey, do you think you need to get your hearing checked?" maybe is a more familiar one!

[3] Psalm 46:10 NIV

Day Ten

LIFE'S TOTAL PACKAGE

Devote yourselves to prayer, being watchful and thankful. And pray for us, too, that God may open a door for our message, so that we may proclaim the mystery of Christ, for which I am in chains. Pray that I may proclaim it clearly, as I should. Be wise in the way you act toward outsiders; make the most of every opportunity. Let your conversation be always full of grace, seasoned with salt, so that you may know how to answer everyone.

—Colossians 4:2-6 NIV

HAVE YOU EVER HEARD SOMEONE REFERRED TO AS THE "TOTAL PACK-age"?[1] Someone who has it all—good looks, smarts, personality, and the list goes on. I want to use this wonderful passage from Paul's letter to the Colossians to describe the term "total package" in a different way. Let's apply it to our lives. Here is what I mean: If we were to live our lives each and every day based upon this passage then our lives would be the "total package." Paul says to:

- Pray
- Be watchful
- Be thankful
- Proclaim the mystery of Christ
- Be wise
- Make the most out of every opportunity
- Have your conversation full of grace and seasoned with salt

If our lives were filled with these qualities and characteristics, then I am here to tell you that we would be well on our way towards perfection as Jesus instructed.[2] So let's discuss each one and how we can make each one a part of our lives.

Pray

A successful walk with the Lord is totally dependent on regular and consistent prayer throughout each day. We need to have that daily conversation with Him, talking with Him about our needs and our concerns. We need to be in humble gratitude for all that He does with a keen appreciation of how awesome He is. We need to seek His forgiveness with a full dose of repentance. Long prayers, short prayers, inside or outside, it does not matter to God. It is that time spent together that is what is so special. Prayer can bring us so much joy, peace, and perseverance. Prayer definitely has an impact on the world around us.

Be Watchful

Scripture talks about being alert, watchful, of sober judgment, and attentive.[3] Why is this so important? We have to be able to determine if something is the will of God. We have to remain fully focused on our faith so we will not slip and go in the wrong direction. We must remain on guard at all times because Satan will deceive and destroy us at every turn. If we are lazy in thought and absent-minded in our plans, then we will find ourselves in a serious state of being.

Be Thankful

While I plan on doing a separate devotional on this, having that sense of gratefulness for all that God has done for us is so vital to our faith journey. I have a good friend who says that one piece of evidence, among several, of being born-again is that strong sense of being truly thankful and that willingness to show it wherever you go.

Proclaim the Mystery of Christ

Said another way, we are to share the Gospel[4] with others. We are to let others know, especially non-believers, that Christ died on the cross for the forgiveness of our sins and He came alive three days later, evidencing our eternal path to heaven to be with Him. That is our duty, that is our responsibility, and that is simply our assignment.

Be Wise

Knowledge does not equate to wisdom. A person can be full of knowledge on many topics and have all the book smarts there are but still lack in the area of wisdom. This lack of wisdom is the inability to make the right choices in life, the failure to recognize that we are sinful creatures and desperately in need of saving, and the refusal to accept the fact that an eternal and sovereign Creator formed this universe and all that is in it by simply making it come into being. This inability, this failure, this refusal are all simply folly and evidence of poor (and deadly) judgment. No wisdom here! But the wise person, my friends, is one who can take that knowledge and put it in perspective in any given situation, thus creating a positive outcome. Sprinkle that with a dose of open-mindedness and a willingness to learn from mistakes, and there you will find a wise person.

Make the Most Out of Every Opportunity

It has been said that life is too short and that we should seize every moment we can. I believe that is a true statement. God created this wonderful world we live in, our wonderful families, and the wonders of nature. God simply wants us to enjoy His creation. We should never let a moment go by without doing that. But better yet, we should never let an opportunity go by to show love, to show compassion for the needy, and to show a heart of integrity and honesty. We should always make the most out of every opportunity, always with an eye on what truly has eternal value.

Have Your Conversation Full of Grace and Seasoned with Salt

We have all said things we later regretted saying. Once that toothpaste is out of the tube, there is no way to put it back in. The book of James devotes much of chapter three to the tongue and mouth, making the analogy of a bit, which can turn a horse, or a small rudder steering a ship. There is a lot of power here. Words that come from our mouths can have a tremendous impact on others, either positive or negative. Paul is saying our words should be full of grace and seasoned with salt. Our words should be positive in all that we do.

Our words should always be encouraging and full of love for everyone we come into contact with. We can make a lasting and good impression on others.

So my friends, do we want to have the kind of life that is rich and full? If we follow Jesus, who says He can give us life to the full, then we can have the "total package" life.

Thought: Which area of your life do you feel like you need to work the most on improving? In what ways can you do that?

Let us pray: Dear Lord, we want to have all of these character traits in our lives. Help us to develop them and live them every day of our lives, full of thanksgiving and grace. Further help us to wisely and attentively choose what we can control in our lives, making the most of every opportunity You place in front of us. We want to share the great news of the Gospel with Your help. We pray this in the most holy name of Your precious Son, Jesus. Amen

---

[1] For you "rasslin" fans, you remember there was a wrestler back in the day who was referred to as the "total package." Anyone remember his name?

[2] See Matthew 5:48.

[3] See Romans 12:2-3, Hebrews 2:1, 1 Peter 5:8 (all NIV).

[4] In my humble opinion, the greatest short sermon was preached by Peter (and others) on the Gospel. See Acts 5:29-32. You just got to love the former disciple and current apostle, Peter!

Day Eleven

THE AROMA OF CHRIST

But thanks be to God, who always leads us as captives in Christ's triumphal procession and uses us to spread the aroma of the knowledge of him everywhere. For we are to God the pleasing aroma of Christ among those who are being saved and those who are perishing. To the one we are an aroma that brings death; to the other an aroma that brings life.

—2 Corinthians 2:14-16a NIV

THE GIRLS IN MY FAMILY (GAYLE, KAT, AND MANDY) LOVE SCENTED CANdles. You can bet at Christmas and on birthdays, somebody is going to get a scented candle, and when one does, the candle is immediately lit. If you ever go into a store that sells scented candles, take a few minutes and look at the names of the scents, and if you want, you can have a pretty good chuckle.[1] Some names of scented candles actually use the word "aroma."

I really like this word, "aroma." It conjures up some pleasing thoughts. For example, if you are a coffee lover, then when you walk into a coffee shop,[2] you probably think *Oh, the rich smell of the various coffees.* How about when you walk into your grandmother's kitchen, and you smell recently baked cakes or you smell the fragrance of a light perfume around your wife's neck? These are all great aromas, are they not?

Paul's use of this word "aroma" is an interesting one. Paul is instructing his readers (which, of course, includes us) to share the sweet smell of the Gospel to everyone and everywhere. We are to present it in a way that is pleasant to those who hear us. Oftentimes people will not be at all receptive to our message if we are bold and brash. We should not be like the man on the street corner with a megaphone in hand, threatening hell and damnation. No, we should present the message in a calm, humble, and loving manner so they will want to experience the sweetness of Jesus.

Paul instructs us to take on the aroma of Christ by displaying all of the wonderful characteristics that Christ showed during His time here on this earth. Becoming more Christlike as we strive towards perfection makes God happy, and it is very much pleasing to Him.

Finally and yet unfortunately, there is a scent that is not good, and it is the aroma of death. Paul refers to those who are perishing, who are unsaved, and those who have not accepted Jesus into their lives. However, there is hope for these folks. If we share the good news of the Gospel in a loving manner and display the wonderful aroma of Jesus around, not just in the community of saved believers but around these non-believers, those perishing, then maybe, just maybe, that tiny seed can be planted. When that seed is planted, then boy, just watch God do some fantastic and amazing watering.

There is that old adage that says, "Stop and smell the roses." This simply means to recognize and appreciate God's goodness in our lives. We need to be so grateful to our Father in heaven for the beauty of life and the sweet aroma of hope that we have because of our Lord and Savior Jesus Christ—the hope of eternal life with Him. So for everyone, we need to stop, breathe in through the nose, and experience that sweet aroma that is of our Jesus.

Thought: Have you ever stopped and thought about the goodness of God and all that He has done in your life? What are some of those things?

Let us pray: Our Father in heaven, thank You for the beauty of this life here on this earth and the promised hope of eternal life with You. Help us to be more Christlike in all that we do and help us also to share the wonderful aroma of the Gospel message so that all can experience Your amazing love and grace. Amen

---

[1] I once saw the name of a scented candle called "FoulSmell." Really?

[2] A shout out to a local coffee shop in a neighboring town of mine—Aromas Uptown Coffee.

Day Twelve

A REVIVAL

*If my people, who are called by my name, will humble them-
selves and pray and seek my face and turn from their wicked
ways, then I will hear from heaven, and I will forgive their sin
and will heal their land.*

—2 Chronicles 7:14 NIV

THERE IS A STORY TOLD OF A GUY BY THE NAME OF LARRY. LARRY HEARD
that there was going to be a revival at the local church, so he decided
to go. At the end of the service, the preacher asked if anyone wanted
to come down front for the preacher to pray for any need they had.
Larry decided to go down front, and when it was his turn, the
preacher asked Larry, "What is it you would like for me to pray for?"

Larry responded, "Preacher, I would like for you to pray for my
hearing." So the preacher got Larry to get close, and he cupped one
hand over one ear and the other hand over the other ear. The

preacher commenced to praying. He probably prayed for at least five minutes.

When the prayer ended, the preacher stepped back, rather proud of his praying abilities, and asked Larry, "How is your hearing now?"

Larry replied, " Preacher, I do not know. It is not scheduled until next Wednesday!"

Maybe just a little miscommunication there.

In all seriousness, I am convinced the medicine this country needs to overcome its many problems is a revival, a great awakening in the spiritual lives of many Americans. Going back to the early 1700s, there have been at least five major revivals in this country led by people like John Wesley, D.L. Moody, Billy Sunday, and Billy Graham. We are certainly due for another one. Why? You may ask. Just look around. There is so much violence, crime, sexual immorality, and division. People have turned away from God in record numbers. Many have left the church. So few truly cherish being in the presence of our holy Creator. Dr. Michael L. Brown said it best in his recent book, *Revival or We Die*[1].

> But God sees the condition of our souls, how we have exchanged the anointing for professionalism, how we have traded dependence on the Spirit for fleshly endeavors, how we have substituted a carnal business approach for our first love devotion. Now is a time to awaken!

Let's look at today's passage. After Solomon finished the Temple, the Lord spoke to him. Does it not sound as if the Lord was calling for a revival—an awakening for the people of Israel? It sure sounds like it to me. So if the Lord wanted it for His people back then, why would He not want it for His people today? I believe He does. I really believe the state of our country simply crushes our Father's heart. He wants us to seek His face and turn from our wicked ways. Just as He promised the Israelites that their land would be healed, I believe the same promise holds true for our land today.

Jesus said, "Because of the increase of wickedness, the love of most will grow cold."[2] There, my friends, is the bottom line. We in this country have lost our love.

We have lost our love for our Heavenly Father and His amazing grace.

We have lost our love for our Savior, Jesus Christ, who died that horrible death for you and for me.

We have allowed this love to be a minor influence in our everyday culture and how we live.

We have lost our love for our neighbors, our friends, and those in need.

We have lost our love for the church.

We have lost our love for the Bible and the richness it brings for hope, peace, and security.

And then we have gone so far as to replace our love.

We have lost our love for what is good and right and replaced it with what is bad and evil.

We have replaced our love for the eternal Gospel with temporary idols and material things.

To return to love is the answer to these problems. Why is love the answer? Because God is love, and He loves us very much. The answer begins with each one of us bringing love back into every facet of our lives. Then I believe a revival will happen—an awakening through God's love that will stir our souls and change the direction that our country is currently headed in. And once that revival begins, then I believe that more and more godly people will rise to face the challenges we have and lead our country straight to our heavenly God who is the creator and sustainer of all that there is.

Thought: What can you do today to help a revival start and spread?

Let us pray: Heavenly Father, we pray for love to be infused in every facet of our beings so that a revival can begin in us and then spread throughout. We humbly pray for that strong desire to see change in our towns, states, and country—that change to seek Your face and turn from our sinful ways. Lord, Your will be done. Amen.

---

[1] Michael L. Brown PhD. *Revival or We Die: A Great Awakening is Our Only Hope.* (Pennsylvania: Destiny Image, 2021), 4.

[2] Matthew 24:12 NIV

Day Thirteen

ENCOURAGEMENT

May our Lord Jesus Christ himself and God our Father, who loved us and by his grace gave us eternal encouragement and good hope, encourage your hearts and strengthen you in every good deed and word.

—2 Thessalonians 2:16-17 NIV

WHY DO YOU THINK ENCOURAGEMENT IS SUCH A GREAT WORD? WHAT better encouragement is there than the eternal encouragement of hope in heaven that God gives us? This is the ultimate encouragement, and with this encouragement comes a better heart and better actions in how we live. We simply are better people for this. We are persuaded to help others with acts of love and compassion. This hope can be the driving force behind all that we do.

Let's dive into what it means to encourage one another. Paul talks a lot about encouragement to others in his letters. For example, he says, "Therefore encourage one another and build each other up, just as in fact you are doing."[1] According to today's passage, we have a mission and an obligation to encourage each other. The first place to start is with the family. Growing up my parents encouraged me a lot whether in athletics or school. They were my constant cheerleaders. Gayle's parents were the same for her as well. We, therefore, took this mode of upbringing in raising Michael and Kat. We, too, were always cheering them on in whatever they were doing and wherever it took us.[2] We must also remember the area with the top priority concerning our spouses and children is their faith. Encouragement is vital in the faith arena.

Encouragement extended outside of our families is also very important. We have friends, believers and non-believers, who can use some of our encouragement as well. So here we go. Let's soak in the eternal encouragement we receive from our God in heaven, which makes us better people as said above, and spread that encouragement to everyone. Let's make the hope of heaven the driving force behind everything we do.

When someone you know is struggling with their faith, encourage them and build them up.

When someone is struggling with a medical crisis, encourage them and build them up.

When someone is struggling with anxiety and stress, encourage them and build them up.

When someone is struggling with an unforgiving heart, encourage them and build them up.

When someone is struggling with a failed relationship, encourage them and build them up.

When someone is struggling with finances, encourage them and build them up.

When someone is struggling with the death of a loved one, encourage them and build them up.

We are to remind them they are children of God and are loved by God. Let them know that you are praying for them

ENCOURAGEMENT

We are not meant to live in isolation. We are not supposed to be on a deserted island. We need community. We should live in a relational environment where we need each other. We should not do life alone. We first need to live a God-filled life, soaking in God's love and grace, and then share that love and grace with everyone. We need to inspire and motivate. We need to uplift and embolden. We need to boost and reassure. We need to praise and energize. This is what encouragement is all about. I believe it is a win-win situation.

Thought: Have you thought of someone recently that you felt needed some encouragement, but you have not reached out yet? What can you do to encourage them?

Let us pray: Lord, as this passage says, You have given us the encouragement of eternity, and with this, we have hope, and with this hope, we have that firm and lasting peace. God, we truly thank You. Lord, also help us to always be an encouragement to others. Amen.

---

[1] 1 Thessalonians 5:11 NIV

[2] Oh, gosh. I can remember on game days (JV football, varsity football, volleyball, basketball, track) with both kids playing, we were scattered everywhere. And if we had to travel 5 miles or one-hundred-and-five miles, it did not matter. Those were some good ole' days. Gayle, we were a little younger then, were we not?

Day Fourteen

TO GOD BE
THE GLORY

*You are worthy, our Lord and God, to receive glory and honor
and power, for you created all things, and by your will they
were created and have their being.*

—Revelation 4:11 NIV

THERE ARE MANY REASONS YOU AND I WERE PUT ON THIS EARTH. BUT
the number one reason is to bring honor and glory to God in all that
we do. So, this devotional is going to be a little different. It contains
almost exclusively quotes from people a whole lot smarter than I am.
Bringing honor and glory to God encompasses how we relate to God
by our praise, our thanksgiving, our reverence, and our trust. These
are some pretty awesome quotes[1] on this principle of bringing honor

and glory to God. They bring out the very nature and character of our Father in heaven. Here we go:

> Our high and privileged calling is to do the will of God in the power of God for the glory of God.
>
> —J.L. Packer

> Our ultimate aim in life is not to be healthy, wealthy, prosperous, or problem free. Our ultimate aim in life is to bring glory to God.
>
> —Anne Graham Lotz

> God is able to take your life, with all the heartache, all of the pain, all of the regret, all of the missed opportunities, and use you for His glory.
>
> —Charles R. Swindoll

> What is the glory of God? It is who God is. It is the essence of His nature; the weight of His importance; the radiance of His splendor; the demonstration of His power; the atmosphere of His presence.
>
> —Rick Warren

> I can't do big things, but I want everything to be for the glory of God.
>
> —Dominic Savio

> If you don't feel strong desires for the manifestation of the glory of God, it is not because you have drunk deeply and are satisfied. It is because you have nibbled so long at the table of the world. Your soul is stuffed with small things, and there is no room for the great.
>
> —John Piper

Daniel gave all the glory to God; he took none of it for himself. There is no limit to what God will do for the believer who will let God have all of the glory.

—Warren W. Wiersbe

The glory of God shines, indeed, in all creatures on high and below, but never more brightly than in the cross.

—John Calvin

Praise and glory to God for whom nothing is too hard.

—Elizabeth Elliot

How to bring glory to God? The Bible's short answer is: by growing more and more like Christ.

—Sinclair B. Ferguson

Live a life of prayer, giving glory to God, and continually listening for His guidance.

—Mary C. Neal

We tend to set up success in Christian work as our purpose, but our purpose should be to display the glory of God in human life, to live a life "hidden with Christ in God" in our everyday human conditions.

—Oswald Chambers

The glory of God, and, as our only means of glorifying Him, the salvation of human souls, is the real business of life.

—C.S. Lewis

So here is what I have to say about this topic—giving God glory takes top billing in our faith journey here on this earth. Why? I believe the answer is simple. God is the Alpha and Omega. He is the creator and sustainer of all that there is. He is the supplier of all our many blessings. He is the source of the forgiveness of our sins through His Son who died for us. He resurrected His Son so eternal life is a reality. God should take top billing in every major aspect of our lives. The very least we can do is honor Him and give Him glory in all that we do by praising Him, thanking Him, and seeking His forgiveness by prayer and in our actions. We should give Him our hearts and make sure He gets all the credit. Amen and amen!

Thought: How do you glorify God? What do you plan to do next to glorify Him?

Let us pray: Our Father in heaven, this day and every day help us to bring You honor and glory in all that we do. When we take You for granted, when our hearts become hard and ungrateful, please remind us of all that You have done for us and that You are most assuredly our God of power and of so much love and grace. Keep us keenly aware of Your sovereignty, Your power, and Your might. Amen.

---

[1] Which, of course, I would like to take credit for these, but that would not be very Christian-like, would it?

Day Fifteen

POSTERITY

Posterity will serve him; future generations will be told about the Lord. They will proclaim his righteousness, declaring to a people yet unborn: He has done it!

—Psalm 22:30-31 NIV[1]

POSTERITY IS DEFINED AS ALL FUTURE GENERATIONS OF PEOPLE—THE descendants of a person. Studies have shown that after just a few generations, our ancestors have been forgotten. This is sad but unfortunately very true. Maybe this is why websites such as Ancestry.com are so popular, but do they tell us about who our ancestors are except for their name, where they were born, and other basic information such as this? I am not being critical of these types of sources[2] of information, but do we really learn who our ancestors were, what they were about, and what made them tick? For some of these places, you can even send in a sample of your DNA so you can learn who all is in your family tree. To be honest, do I really want to know how many criminals, scoundrels, rascals, and crooks are in my ancestry line?[3] I heard a man say once, "I could not afford an ancestry DNA kit, so I announced that I had won the lottery, and I soon found out who all of my relatives were."

In Psalm 22, we find David crying out to the Lord, pleading with Him to rescue him from his enemies and ease the troubles that he is experiencing. Then David realizes that his Lord has rescued him, and David offers his praise and thanks. But David goes one step further, I believe, and encourages his readers and future readers to fully realize just how awesome his Lord, our Lord, really is. Verse 31 says, "they will proclaim His righteousness." Future generations will come to know the Lord.

This passage for today is so directly opposite to the above studies showing the lack of ancestry knowledge after a few generations. For us and all future generations will not forget our Lord who created the heavens and the earth, who shaped the lives of the likes of Abraham, Moses, and David, and who sacrificed His Son on the cross and brought Him back to life three days later.

Since we have not forgotten who our Lord is:

- We, therefore, know that our Lord is our strength

- We, therefore, know that our Lord will protect us

- We, therefore, know that our Lord always hears our cries for help

- We, therefore, know that our Lord will always satisfy us

As a result, we:

- Fear and revere Him
- Honor Him
- Praise Him

There is a companion passage found in the book of Psalms, and it reads as follows:

> In the beginning you laid the foundations of the earth, and the heavens are the work of your hands. They will perish, but you remain; they will wear out like a garment. Like clothing you will change them and they will be discarded. But you remain the same, and your years will never end. The children of your servants will live in your presence; their descendants will be established before you.[4]

God is constant and never changing. As the above psalmist says, "He remains the same." For everyone, all descendants and all children will live in the presence of the Lord. Everyone will know that He is Lord.

No need to buy a DNA kit. We know who our Father in heaven is because we are His children. We know who our family is because we are believers in the body of Christ. God is the creator and sustainer of all life and deserves all honor and glory and will be glorified by all creatures forever and ever.

Everyone will proclaim God's goodness and righteousness! Everyone will praise His name! Everyone will say, "Yes! He has done it!"

Thought: Do you know who God really is? Do you know the fact that He is all-knowing, all-powerful, and all-present—the beginning and the end?

Let us pray: Dear Heavenly Father, we give You thanks for Your greatness. We give You thanks for being there for all generations before and after us until the end of time, allowing so many people to partake of Your goodness and mercy. Oh, what a wonderful Father You are! Amen.

[1] FYI: Psalm 22 bears a relationship with Jesus on the cross. Many people believe that when Jesus says, "My God, my God, why have you forsaken me," he is quoting from the first verse of this psalm.

[2] Now, if you are a big fan and user of these, please accept my apologies!

[3] Whoops, sorry again.

[4] Psalm 102:25-27 NIV

Day Sixteen

ALMOST CHRISTIAN

Not everyone who says to me, 'Lord, Lord,' will enter the king-
dom of heaven, but only the one who does the will of my Father
who is in heaven. Many will say to me on that day, 'Lord, Lord
did we not prophesy in your name and in your name drive out
demons and in your name perform many miracles?' Then I
will tell them plainly, 'I never knew you. Away from me, you
evildoers!'

—Matthew 7:21-23 NIV

Do YOU EVER FEEL FRUSTRATED BY THE WORD "ALMOST"? IT MEANS NOT
quite, very nearly, close to, not far from, verging on. Here are some
familiar phrases that maybe you have heard or used:

- "I almost made my sales quota."
- "How far, Daddy?"
  "Almost there."
- A waitress asks if you're ready to order. "Almost."
- "Honey, are you ready?"
  "Almost"

Almost—we are coming close but not quite there yet. As the old phrase goes, "Close but no cigar."[1] But as they say, "Close only counts in horseshoes and hand grenades." The word "almost" sometimes signifies that we want to delay something. That we are not quite ready to cross the finish line. That we are not ready to make that commitment. Just not ready. Sometimes we are ready to just take the consolation prize, the runner-up trophy, or the bronze or silver medal. Not the effort we want to put into it. Almost, almost, almost.

Therefore, the question I am posing to you, readers is are you willing to accept the title of "Almost Christian"? I hope not!

In Acts 26, there is a great story about the Apostle Paul's encounter with King Agrippa (King of Judea). Paul was in prison in a place called Caesarea. He first appeared before Festus,[2] a Roman governor where Paul pled not guilty to the charges levied against him and requested that he be allowed to appear before King Caesar. This request was granted, but in the meantime, King Agrippa and his sister, Bernice, came to pay their respects to Governor Festus. Festus tells King Agrippa that he has this guy named Paul, who the Jewish leaders want to be tried and put to death. He told the king that he originally thought the charges were serious, but it turns out they are only based on religion and some dead guy named Jesus. Festus told the king that he did not know what to do with Paul, and the king said that he would talk with him.

Paul continues to plead his case in Acts 26 before the king with a mighty powerful sermon, that is very much worth reading. When Paul was finished, King Agrippa responded, "[Paul], you *almost* persuade me to become a Christian" (emphasis mine).[3] See, King

Agrippa was evidently moved by Paul's powerful and persuasive argument in support of the Gospel, but he unfortunately did not want to make the commitment, and he walked away from it.

We have to be very careful here. We do not want to rely totally on being kind and considerate people, coming to church every Sunday, and helping out at the local soup kitchen. While all of these things are good, they are not enough to get us into heaven. I believe that one problem in our society is that there are a lot of people walking around professing to be Christians when in fact they are not. So here are some things that I believe are absolutely essential to be a real Christian—a born-again Christian—and not an almost Christian (and this list is a short list out of a much longer list):

1. You must *trust* in the fact that Jesus died on the cross for the forgiveness of your sins.

2. You must *trust* in the fact that Jesus came back alive three days later so you can have eternal life in heaven.

3. You must *trust* in the fact that the process of forgiveness is a two-way street. God forgives, and to seek His forgiveness, you must confess your sins, repent of your sins, and seek change.

4. You must *trust* in the fact that the Bible is God's word and immerse yourself in it on a daily basis.

5. You must *trust* in the fact that God's Holy Spirit will come into your heart and guide and direct you every single day of your life if you simply allow Him to.

6. You must *trust* in the fact that God is full of profound grace and mercy, and He enjoys showering that grace and mercy on you.

We do not want to be half-hearted Christians. We do not want to be double-life Christians, professing one thing and doing something else. We do not want to live life just going through the motions, waiting for a time when it is convenient. We do not want to be Almost Christian.

When we die and we are standing before Jesus, we do not want Him to say, "I never knew you! Away from me!" Oh, no! We do not want that! Absolutely not! We do not want to be like King Agrippa, who was moved by Paul's words but did not want to fully step into faith. No, here is what we want: "Come on in! Welcome to Paradise, my good and faithful servant! Glad you are here!"

Thought: This is a strong question but a most serious one! Are you an Almost Christian? If your answer is yes, then would you like to be a real Christian?

Let us pray: Our Savior Jesus, help us be firm in our faith, truly committed to You. Help us to follow You in all that we do, surrendering our lives to You. Thank You for dying for us and coming to life for us. Amen.

---

[1] In the early 1900's, cigars were given as prizes at fairs.

[2] Remember the old television show *Gunsmoke* and the character Festus, who was the Sheriff's deputy? I wonder if the writers of this show named this character after Festus, the Roman governor?

[3] Acts 26:28 NKJV

Day Seventeen

TRAGEDY

Consider it pure joy, my brothers and sisters, whenever you face trials of many kinds, because you know that the testing of your faith produces perseverance. Let perseverance finish its work so that you may be mature and complete, not lacking anything.

—James 1:2-4 NIV

God is our refuge and strength, an ever-present help in trouble.

—Psalm 46:1 NIV

MY HEART IS HEAVY AND ACHING TODAY. ABOUT THREE HOURS BEFORE the time of this writing, Gayle and I learned that some very dear and close friends of ours lost their home to a fire. It burned to the ground due to the effects of Hurricane Ian, resulting in an electrical fire. The pain and sorrow they are going through at this moment is beyond my comprehension, but the good news is their faith is very strong, and they are praising God for the fact that neither was home at the time, and their beloved dog was rescued from the burning house by a neighbor. Gayle and I have been communicating with them this morning through texts, and while they are completely devastated by this horrible tragedy, they have found themselves still thankful to God for saving them and their family dog.

What do we do when tragedy, trials, illness, and death knock at our door? What do we do when life hits us with a punch to the gut and we double up in pain? What do we do when everything around us seems so unfair and one-sided? What do we do? We pray, and we pray, and we pray. And we ask others to pray for us. And our friends and family ask others to pray. We go to the God of all creation and ask Him for strength. We ask Him for peace and comfort. We ask Him for recovery. We ask Him to give us endurance. We ask Him for the perseverance, as James says, to get us through to the point where we will not be lacking for anything.[1]

As soon as Gayle and I learned of this horrible news, we commenced contacting friends, our prayer warriors, across the state to pray for this couple who lost their home. I even had one friend contacted for prayer respond back to me, and he thanked me for asking him to pray. Wow! He said his reason for thanking me is that he considers it a blessing when he is asked to pray for someone.

During our limited time this morning texting with this hurting couple, we asked the following question: "What do people do in times like these who do not know the Lord's peace?" That is a question that I have asked many times. It is a mystery to me when a nonbeliever experiences a tragedy—where do they go? What or whom do they rely on when disaster strikes? What is out there when someone's life is turned upside down with devastation? What eases their pain when hardship tears at the core of their being? Maybe they turn to things of this world that will not give them any lasting satisfaction, things that can only ease the hurt for just a little bit of time.

What can Gayle and I learn from what our dear friends have experienced and the journey they have to walk through in the days and weeks ahead? It is this. We have a great God who can and will overcome any problems in our lives. We have a great God who reminds us He is the God of strength and comfort who can and will give us peace in times of trouble. We have a great God who also reminds us that life is not going to be easy and that mishaps and misfortune will be so difficult to endure, but we have Him on our side, holding our hand every step of the way.

Finally, we have a great God who wants us to share His love with others, especially those who do not know Him. He wants us to let others know that He is a fortress in times of tragedy, and if only we turn to Him, then He can get us through. While the pain will really hurt, He will ease the pain. While the heartache will crush our souls, He will lift us up to overcome. While the stress and anxiety will be overwhelming, He will grant us peace and calm.

All praise and honor are yours, Lord!

JB and M, we love you and are praying for you![2]

Thought: Where do you turn when life gets rocky?

Let us pray: Lord, You are our rock and our redeemer. You are our strength and source of peace and comfort. Help us always to turn to You when life gets rough, knowing that with You we can get through, even though it is very difficult, whatever is in our way. We give You thanks, Lord. Amen

---

[1] See James 1:2-4 (NIV).

[2] They are doing great and have built another house.

Day Eighteen

THE RAPTURE

According to the Lord's word, we tell you that we who are still alive, who are left until the coming of the Lord, will certainly not precede those who have fallen asleep. For the Lord himself will come down from heaven, with a loud command, with the voice of the archangel and with the trumpet call of God, and the dead in Christ will rise first. After that, we who are still alive and are left will be caught up together with them in the clouds to meet the Lord in the air. And so we will be with the Lord forever. Therefore encourage one another with these words.

—1 Thessalonians 4:15-18 NIV

DID YOU KNOW THE WORD RAPTURE DOESN'T APPEAR ANYWHERE IN THE Bible? However, its definition, "to be caught up," does, as you can see from today's passage. So when we talk about the rapture in reference to the end times, what are we talking about? What is the rapture? In simple terms, it is an event when Jesus comes for His Church, which is the body of believers. I will tell you now this will be a spectacular and amazing event.

Let me put things in perspective so hopefully when you end this devotion, you will have a fairly good idea of what this event is all about. I am going to break it down into three categories.

1. The Timing of the Rapture

Please allow me first to explain what the End of Times is so the timing of the Rapture will make more sense. The End of Times will involve the following major events:

1. Rise of the Antichrist through Satan

2. Seven years of the Great Tribulation, some of which will involve horrible and catastrophic events

3. The Second Coming of Jesus

4. Jesus' 1,000-year reign on earth

5. The merging of the New Heaven and New Earth

I realize that the above may not make a lot of sense, and quite frankly, it is due to the fact that it requires a full and complete study of the End of Times and the Book of Revelation.

The majority of scholars believe that the Rapture will happen immediately preceding the beginning of the Great Tribulation and the Rise of the Antichrist. Some scholars, however, believe that it will take place three-and-a-half years into the Great Tribulation, and others believe it will be at the end of the Great Tribulation. I fully agree with the majority that it will take place at the beginning, and it just makes more sense that way.

2. What is the Rapture, and how will it work?

First of all, the Rapture is not to be confused with Jesus' Second Coming. The Rapture is Jesus coming for His saints, and the Second Coming is Jesus coming to earth with His saints[1] from heaven. Jesus will come down, but I do not believe very far because His saints will rise and be caught up in the clouds to meet the Lord in the air. He is bringing his saints, dead and alive, home. I believe that the heavens will open up, and there is Jesus. The dead in Christ will rise first and be reunited with their souls, and living believers will go next. When this happens, we will all, dead and alive, have our new, resurrected bodies. This event will happen so quickly. In an instant, the dead (in whatever form they are in — in the ground or in an urn) will rise first; those who are still alive will rise next. Paul tells us it will happen "in a flash, in a twinkling of an eye."[2]

3. The Purpose for the Rapture

As stated above, the primary purpose for the Rapture is Jesus bringing His Church home. His Church comprises all believers, dead and living. But I believe there are two other purposes that can be equally important. First of all, I believe that God will be protecting His living believers from the horrors of the Great Tribulation. You must recognize that God is bringing His judgment on the sinful and rebellious earth. He is going to do so with plagues, natural disasters, and horrors of many kinds. He is not going to allow His faithful to experience this, and thus, His faithful will go with Jesus prior to this event. Secondly, as I stated before, when Jesus returns at His Second Coming, Paul tells us He will be coming with His holy ones (saints), and this means all of His saints.[3] He simply wants all of His saints to be with Him when He makes His triumphal and glorious return to earth. What better way to do it than to be present with His Church?

Before I close this devotional, some of my readers may be asking themselves, "Why do a devotion on the Rapture?" First of all, a study of the End of Times and the Book of Revelation, the last book of the New Testament, is very important to everyone's faith journey. Having a knowledge and understanding of how matters will end, along with the holy return of our Lord and Savior at His Second Coming, is essential to the Christian walk. I could have selected any major event in the End-of-Times scenario, but I chose the Rapture as the perfect prelude to the End of Times. It is like the pre-game festivities or pre-game analysis leading up to the championship game. So I hope I have "whet your appetites" to begin your own study of the End of Times and the Book of Revelation. Get yourself a good commentary or study guide and dig in and, for sure, don't be scared. No reason to be scared. This book offers so much hope and peace. You will find comfort in your study.

Thought: How do you feel when you think about the end times? How can you invite God's peace in as you study the end times?

Let us pray: Dear Holy Jesus, help us be in much sacred anticipation and joyful hope for Your bringing Your church home with You. Keep us watchful and attentive always. Amen

---

[1] Jude verse 14b (NIV) uses the words "holy ones."

[2] 1 Corinthians 15:52 NIV

[3] See 1 Thessalonians 3:13.

Day Nineteen

GOD LOVES THE
SINNER

And Saul approved of their killing him.

—Acts 8:1a NIV

But Saul began to destroy the church. Going from house to house, he dragged off both men and women and put them in prison.

—Acts 8:3 NIV

Meanwhile, Saul was still breathing out murderous threats against the Lord's disciples. He went to the high priest and asked him for letters to the synagogues in Damascus, so that if he found any there who belonged to the Way,[1] whether men or women, he might take them as prisoners to Jerusalem. As he neared Damascus on his journey, suddenly a light from heaven flashed around him. He fell to the ground and heard a voice say to him, "Saul, Saul, why do you persecute me?" "Who are you, Lord?" Saul asked. "I am Jesus, whom you are persecuting," he replied. "Now get up and go into the city, and you will be told what you must do."

—Acts 9:1-6 NIV

BEFORE BECOMING THE APOSTLE PAUL AND WRITING 13 (OR 14) BOOKS in the New Testament, Saul was an evil man on a mission. He was relentless in persecuting the early Christians. He would capture them and either put them in prison or resort to murdering them. He approved of the killing of Stephen (Acts 8:1a above and Day One). He was a modern-day Adolph Hitler or Osama bin Laden. Saul was simply the worst of the worst. He was one bad dude!

When I think about Saul, I remember the saying that "God loves the sinner but hates the sin."[2] I think there is some truth in that statement. Let's explore that for a minute and how we can relate it to the story of Paul. Let's first remember that God really hates sin. How do we know that? Simple. God sent His only Son Jesus to the cross to die so that our sins would be forgiven. It was not a normal death either. It was a horrific death. It started off with brutal floggings and beatings coupled with humiliating insults and treatment by the Roman guards. Then Jesus was nailed to the wooden cross at His arms and feet, resulting in excruciating pain, loss of blood, and loss of oxygen because of the inability to breathe. Crucifixion on the cross was the most barbaric manner of death known in that time. Jesus was on the cross for six hours. There had to be a sacrifice, and Jesus was the one to do it. Jesus took on what we deserved. While Jesus did this out of His love for us, it was God who caused it to happen. Sin brings death, and Jesus died for us. Jesus, in all of His perfection, took on our sins. You see, in order to be a part of God's family, in order to approach our heavenly Father who is holy, pure, and perfect, we had to be cleansed, and it was done with the blood of Jesus. Sin is simply incompatible with a divine and righteous God.

So how does Saul (Paul) on the road to Damascus fit into all this? Remember our statement above that God loves the sinner. God definitely loves the sinner. He loves everyone as He has created everyone. So, in God's infinite love and grace, He took this villain who was creating havoc for His early Church and killing His beloved creation and took him in. He was simply shown the mercy and grace of God. Paul admitted to being the worst of sinners in the following passage of scripture (and what a great passage this is):

> Here is a trustworthy saying that deserves full acceptance: Christ Jesus came into the world to save sinners—of whom I am the worst. But for that very reason I was shown mercy so that in me, the worst of sinners, Christ Jesus might display his immense patience as an example for those who would believe in him and receive eternal life. (1 Tim. 1:15-16 NIV)

Paul acknowledges that he is "the worst of sinners." Did that matter to God? Nope! God said He was going to take "the worst of sinners" and make him a great man of faith, a man who God would use to author many great books of the Bible. Why? It is because of love. It is because of unending grace and mercy. Jesus died for the ungodly, the wicked, His enemies, you and me. He died while we were still sinners.[3]

So there is hope for everyone. Jesus will wash our smelly, dirty feet if we just allow him to.[4] Our sin was no match for the sacrifice that was shown on the cross for you and me. Yes, God hates sin but loves the sinner. And I am sure Paul would definitely agree.

Moral of the story: No one is too sinful to be saved!

Thought: Is it hard for you to comprehend just how great God's love is for us? If so, why is it so hard?

Let us pray: Our Father in heaven, we give You thanks and praise for Your unending love that You have for us. We are so unworthy; we are so sinful. But You still love us anyway. Your love is so great that You allowed Your precious Jesus to suffer for us on the cross. Keep our hearts eternally grateful for Your love. Amen

---

[1] The early Christians were known as the Way.

[2] Some people credit this statement to St. Augustine.

[3] See Romans 5:8 (NIV).

[4] See *Just Me, Lucy, and the Lord,* Day 23.

Day Twenty

NO OTHER GODS

And God spoke all these words: "I am the Lord your God, who brought you out of Egypt, out of the land of slavery. You shall have no other gods before me. You shall not make for yourself an image in the form of anything in heaven above or on the earth beneath or in the waters below. You shall not bow down to them or worship them; for I, the Lord your God, am a jealous God, punishing the children for the sin of the parents to the third and fourth generation of those who hate me, but showing love to a thousand generations of those who love me and keep my commandments."

—Exodus 20:1-6 NIV

I HEARD A STORY ONCE WHERE A HUSBAND AND WIFE CAME TO CHURCH after a lengthy absence, and after church, the pastor came up to the husband and said, "Jim, so glad you and Mary are here. I have not seen you in quite some time."

Jim replied, "Yes, I know that, but I do want you to know, Reverend, that Mary and I keep the Ten Commandments."

The pastor responded, "That is so good, Jim."

Jim stated back, "Yes I keep four, and Mary keeps six!"

Well, I believe that God intended for us to keep all ten commandments, right?

Our passage for today consists of the first and second commandments. They are really connected together, and if you think about it, we probably violate these two commandments the most. Here is what I mean.

We all unfortunately put many "gods" ahead of our heavenly God. Oftentimes, our heavenly God is down the list of what we place as important in our lives. Sadly, we allow God to take a backseat to what we devote our time, energy, wealth, and even our thoughts to. We put God on the shelf and take Him off only if it is convenient or when things get rough, saying, "Oh God, I need you! Help me, Lord!" Now we are not constructing golden cows to worship as Moses' people were doing, but we do have those things in our lives that are pretty dang important to us. While we do not want to admit it, we do engage in some form of idol-worshiping. So I am going to provide what I believe to be a common list of our "gods," and see if any of you can relate.

Work

There is nothing wrong with a good work ethic. Working hard and being loyal and devoted to our jobs is very admirable. "Earn your keep" is one of the things that has made America great. I am so fortunate that my entire family has always been dependable and valued assets to their respective places of employment. But here is where the problem lies:

- When we place greater emphasis on our jobs than on our relationship with God

- When we work that Sunday morning to get caught up instead of going to church

- When we sleep in a little later because we put in a few extra hours the day before, thereby not having some quiet devotional time that morning

- When our time is always spent on job productivity, and we don't stop throughout the day to say a quick little prayer to our Heavenly Father

I currently have a little over two years before I retire. I am already concerned about not having the job I have currently when the retirement age begins. I keep telling myself, and I am working through this, when I retire, I will have plenty of time to serve the Lord, something I have not done enough of.

Family

Please allow me to state right off the bat that I love my family so very much, and I have been truly blessed by everyone in my family, beginning with Gayle, my wife of over 46 years, all the way down to my three-and-a-half-year-old grandson, son, daughter, and daughter-in-law. There is nothing that I would not do for them. I have talked about my family a lot in this book. They are mighty important to me. Once again, however, we cannot place family above God.

Let's look at family this way. We are commanded in scripture to take care of our families, honor our mothers and fathers, and raise our children in a Christian environment. I think we should be able to strike more of a balance between family and God but again, not placing family above God. I believe it was best said when Jesus was asked about the greatest commandment, and He said, "Love the Lord with all heart, soul, and mind." Jesus also said the second greatest commandment is to love our neighbor as ourselves.[1]

Wouldn't it be fair to say that our families, in some way, are also our neighbors? Love the Lord, love our family, take care of our family, and keep things in perspective.

Entertainment

Now, I really like a good college football or basketball game, especially if it involves Clemson, but here is what I have thought about many times: In any given year, many fans spend hours on end traveling to and from these games and several hours in the game. Now here is what I wonder: Does the average fan spend the same amount of time with God or for their local church as they do for their favorite team? What about time spent on social media, watching television, or listening to music? Does this time far exceed time spent reading the Bible, praying, and meditating? This one is a no-brainer. Entertainment is simply taking a place above God, and this should not be.

Wealth/Material Things

Jesus said it best when He talked about money. He said one cannot serve two masters—money and God.[2] That is so true. How many times do we fail to give to the Lord what is rightly His? We will hoard our money under the pretense of savings or future retirement. Or we will purchase something that we really do not need instead of giving it to a worthwhile cause. Jesus also said in this passage trying to serve two masters will result in loving one and hating the other or being devoted to one and despising the other. Oh gosh! Heaven forbid we make the wrong choice here!

Let me say this as a closing remark. God has never intended for us not to work hard, not love our family, not go to football games, and not accumulate wealth. These are good things and certainly alright to have and to do. God is fine with that. But we must remember this—that all of these things will not get us into heaven. They simply will not nor will we be able to take any of this with us when we die.

The only absolute truth for eternal life in heaven is a relationship with Jesus, our Lord and Savior Christ. Again, we simply need to always place God first in our lives and not allow anything, our "gods," to stand in the way of having that loving relationship with our heavenly Creator. As my family likes to say, "That's a fact, Jack!"

Thought: Have you ever focused on what has temporary value in your life and what has eternal value? What "gods" do you struggle with putting above God?

Let us pray: Lord, help us always to keep You number one in our lives. When we slip, when we treasure something in place of You, please turn us around and remind us that You created us, that You provide for us, and by Your grace, we have been saved by Your Son, Jesus. Please allow that to be our focus, our priority in life. Amen

---

[1] Matthew 22:37-40 NIV

[2] See Matthew 6:24 (NIV).

Day Twenty-One

THE HOLY SPIRIT

But the fruit of the Spirit is love, joy, peace, forbearance, kindness, goodness, faithfulness, gentleness, and self-control.

—Galatians 5:22-23 NIV

[Jesus said], "And I will ask the Father, and he will give you another advocate to help you and be with you forever—the Spirit of truth."

—John 14:16-17a NIV

And hope does not put us to shame, because God's love has been poured out into our hearts through the Holy Spirit, who has been given to us.

—Romans 5:5 NIV

WHEN I WAS GROWING UP AND HEARD IN CHURCH REFERENCES TO THE Holy Ghost, I felt a little creeped out, I must admit. The preacher would be talking about Jesus and His love, and then there is some mention of a "ghost." Whoa! Come on now! I guess back then the King James version of the Bible was primarily used in churches, and it is this translation that references the Holy Ghost and not Holy Spirit. I just kinda' like the use of the Holy Spirit.

Before any deep discussion can take place about the Holy Spirit, the first question that must be asked and answered is "Who is the Holy Spirit?" The Holy Spirit is a person, co-equal with God and Jesus but also a separate and distinct member of the Holy Trinity along with God and Jesus. The Holy Spirit is mentioned throughout scripture, Old and New Testament. The very second verse of the Bible reads "… the Spirit of God was hovering over the waters."[1] The Holy Spirit was active in many people's lives in scripture, but the best part of it all is that the Holy Spirit is active in the lives of every — yes, every — believer. When one is born again by accepting Jesus as Lord and Savior, God's Spirit takes up residence in the person's heart and mind. Now, does the Holy Spirit shy away from a non-believer? I do not think so. I believe that the Holy Spirit is instrumental in a person coming to Christ. But the focus of this devotional will be looking at some of the awesome things the Holy Spirit can do for a believer.

We must remember that the attributes of God are the same for the Holy Spirit. Certainly, too, the power of the Holy Spirit is, of course, unlimited because once again, He is God. That is why I noted the above three passages of scripture which each gives a different take on what the Holy Spirit can do. So let's dive into what this member of the Holy Trinity, however often forgotten, can do for us, and it is all backed up by scripture. I am going to discuss three ways, but there are many more.

He helps us to be more like Christ.

Once we become a believer, we go through and continuously go through a sanctification process, which sets us apart and makes us holy. In other words, He makes us more like Christ. In this process, we experience the Fruits of the Spirit.[2] We have more love, joy, peace, forbearance, kindness, goodness, faithfulness, gentleness, and self-control.

He helps us to spread the Gospel.

Jesus commanded His followers[3] to go "to the ends of the earth" and spread the Gospel. This applies to us today. The help we get from the Holy Spirit is boldness, the courage to preach the Good News, the knowledge of what to say, and the desire to spread the Word. Jesus said in Acts 1:8 that when the Holy Spirit comes, power will be received. I liken this to a rowboat versus a motorized speedboat. The rowboat is powered by human strength and energy. It can't go very far or fast. But with a speedboat, there is power from the engine to get you far and fast. The Holy Spirit powers our boat to help us spread the Gospel and, really, help us in every aspect of our lives.

He helps us with our prayer life.

We all struggle from time to time in our prayer life. We oftentimes do not know what to pray for or we pray for practically the same things each time we pray. But help is on the way! We have the Holy Spirit who knows our weaknesses and one of our weaknesses can be prayer.[4] So, when we find ourselves in some sort of prayer rut, we simply go to the Holy Spirit and seek His guidance and direction. Seek His power. I think when we resort to the Holy Spirit, we probably will be amazed at the help we can get.

If we will work at allowing the Holy Spirit, God's Spirit, to work mightily in our lives, then a change is on the way. A sure change. A wonderful change.

Thought: How do you see the Holy Spirit working in your life?

Let us pray: Holy Spirit, please help us to rely on Your awesome power and strength. Never let us forget that You came to live within us once we believed in Jesus as our Lord and Savior. Guide and direct us always to seek to do our Father's will, and in all that we do, we do it to bring Him all honor and glory. Amen.

---

[1] Genesis 1:2 NIV

[2] See Galatians 5:22-23 (NIV).

[3] See Acts 1:8 (NIV).

[4] See Romans 8:26-27 (NIV).

Day Twenty-Two

GIVING THANKS

Rejoice always, pray continually, give thanks in all circumstances; for this is God's will for you in Christ Jesus.

—1 Thessalonians 5:16-18 NIV

ONE OF MY FAVORITE QUESTIONS TO ASK IS "WHEN YOU WAKE UP IN THE morning and all that you have, your total existence consists of what you had thanked God for, what would you have?"[1] This could be a wake-up call for many of us. Think about it. How often do we give thanks to God for all that He has given us, for the many blessings we receive each and every day, and for the life and sacrifice of His Son, Jesus?

Giving thanks is a core lesson in living life. Gratitude is simply a condition of the heart. When we live a life of thankfulness, when we show gratitude in all aspects of our lives, then the quality of our lives will dramatically improve. We will be driven towards being better stewards of what we have. We will be driven towards a keener awareness of the needs of others. We will be driven towards a desire to share the good news of the Gospel.

I know what you are thinking. What about those times when things are not going very well in our lives? How can we be thankful then? Paul tells us in all things God works for our good if we love him and are called according to his purpose.[2] He says in all things, which would mean good times and bad times. We typically do not thank God for the problem we are facing, certainly not. We thank Him for how He sustains us and helps us through the problem.

I love the story that is told by Corrie ten Boom in her book, *The Hiding Place*.[3] During World War II, Corrie and her sister, Betsie, were prisoners in a German prison camp. They were imprisoned for helping Jews escape from Nazi Germany. The barracks where Corrie and Betsie were housed had a severe flea infestation problem. One day Betsie told Corrie that she did not think she could go on much longer because of the flea problem. Corrie responded by telling Betsie that they needed to thank God for the fleas. Of course, Betsie thought her sister had gone crazy and asked her to explain. Corrie proceeded to tell Betsie that because of the fleas, the ruthless and abusive German guards refused to come into their barracks. Corrie knew to follow the instructions that we are to "always give thanks to God the Father for everything."[4]

When we have a truly grateful heart, we then become a positive influence in our homes, workplaces, and neighborhoods. I believe the foundational key here is humility. A grateful person takes no one or nothing for granted and never believes that they are better than others. If pride seeps in, then the sense of gratitude will start to diminish. Being grateful starts with the little things. If you cannot be grateful for the small things in life, then how can you be grateful for the big things. I have a pet peeve, one among many sadly, and it goes like this: You are in traffic, and someone needs to pull out in your lane of travel. So you stop and motion for them to pull out in front of you, and they do so without the first sign of appreciation. Not the first wave or any kind of gesture. Nothing! The small things, my friends.

Gratitude all starts with God. We should every day thank Him for the many blessings, for His protection, and for His love and grace. When we do, we will do it in prayer to our Heavenly Father, and we will rejoice. Oh yes, with a joyful and glad heart! And the next time we are trying to pull out in traffic, and someone lets us in, then we will certainly show them thanks and also give thanks to God for that kind person.

Thought: When was the last time you stopped and truly gave thanks to God for all that He has done for you?

Let us pray: Dear heavenly and most gracious God, we give You thanks for all of our many blessings that You have given us. We are so unworthy of Your love and grace, yet You provide and provide beyond measure. Keep our hearts grateful and help us never to forget that all that we have has come from You. Amen

---

[1] I would like to take ownership of this question, but I cannot. For the life of me, I cannot remember where I saw or heard this question in the past.

[2] See Romans 8:28.

[3] Publisher: Chosen Books

[4] See Ephesians 5:20 (NIV).

Day Twenty-Three

STRENGTH AND COURAGE

No one will be able to stand against you all the days of your life. As I was with Moses, so I will be with you; I will never leave you nor forsake you. Be strong and courageous, because you will lead these people to inherit the land I swore to their ancestors to give them.

—Joshua 1:5-6 NIV

TODAY'S PASSAGE CONTAINS THE INITIAL INSTRUCTION GOD GAVE JOSHUA who succeeded Moses as leader of the Israelites. God specifically tells Joshua to be strong and courageous because God is with him. Now, Joshua is not the only person God has said to be "strong and courageous." As believers, God reminds us of that every day, and the key is that God is always with us.

What does strength mean? What does courage mean? I went to Google[1], and it appears that courage and strength are somewhat synonymous with each other. Meaning, courage is defined as "strength in the face of pain or grief," As well as "strength to venture, persevere, and withstand when danger, fear, or difficulty appears". Hmm … This unfortunately brings about a confession that I will just have to go ahead and admit now. I do not like heights. I am really scared of them. For example, I cannot watch a movie when someone is standing on a ledge of a high-rise building.[2] Nope, can't do it!

There are times when there is that fear or some obstacle that we cannot seem to get around. Oftentimes we are confronted with illness and even death or just a problem that seems unsolvable. The good news, no, the great news, is that we have a Father in heaven who is in control and will provide the strength, the courage, to face that giant, that mountain, that fear, that peril, and bring us home safely all through the awesome power of His Holy Spirit.

We have all either read or know personally stories of heroics where men and women have faced dangers of whatever kind and have survived by strength and courage. Stories of rescues by firefighters and first responders. Stories of survival in the midst of natural disasters. Stories of countless hours spent to treat and heal people in the face of potential exposure during our recent and unprecedented pandemic. Headline news that makes us all proud as we shout in applause and thanksgiving. But most of us are not going to face the armies in battle that Joshua faced. No, where most of us will need the strength and courage to endure are in the small things in life. While extremely important, they are not going to be on the grand stage for all to see. Mother Teresa has been quoted as saying, "Be faithful in small things because it is in them that your strength lies."[3] Some examples of maybe when you and I should pray for God's strength and courage are when we want to:

- Stand up for what is right no matter the consequences

- Love the unlovable

- Speak out for truth when truth is not popular

- Go after dreams and goals, even when failures creep in

- Step out of our comfort zones

- Be bold in faith in every circumstance

- Most importantly, trust in a faithful and dependable God

We must never forget that our God assures us He is always with us and He will give us the strength and courage to face whatever challenge comes our way. When life gets tough, and it has and will get tough, remember God loves us, is with us, and will provide everything we need to handle and persevere through the storms of life and maybe even those "scary heights."

Thought: What areas of life do you need more of God's strength and courage? How can you receive it?

Let us pray: Dear Lord, we pray for strength and courage so we can get through life's struggles. Please remind us constantly that Your Holy Spirit will never leave us nor forsake and that He is by our side every step of the way. Thank you. Amen

---

[1] Have you ever wondered where Google got its name? I do not know, but if I had to guess, I would say they probably "googled" it!

[2] Did anyone see the movie *Mission Impossible: Ghost Protocol,* released in 2011, where Tom Cruise is seen hanging by one gloved hand outside on a window from the world's tallest skyscraper, Burj Khalifa, in Dubai, United Arab Emirates. It was absolutely crazy! I closed my eyes the entire time in that movie theater. And I think I even slumped down in the seat for extra protection, all the while Michael and Kat were saying, "Really, Dad?"

[3] www.azquotes.com

Day Twenty-Four

THE SERVANT

For even the Son of Man did not come to be served, but to serve, and to give his life as a ransom for many.

—Mark 10:45 NIV

IMAGINE SOMEONE WHO IS THE FIRST TO STEP IN WHEN SOMEONE NEEDS help. Someone who never has any expectation of anything in return. Maybe you're thinking of a particular person in your own life. Or maybe you are that person! I like to call this person a servant. This is an area where I struggle at times. But I must remember, and you must remember, we have been commanded by Jesus to feed the hungry, provide drink to the thirsty, invite the stranger in, clothe the naked, look after the sick, and visit those in prison.[1]

Without question, Jesus was and is the ultimate servant. Let's look at a few examples of Jesus in action in scripture and then look at Jesus in action today.

- Jesus fed the five thousand (Matthew 14:13-21).

- Jesus healed ten men with leprosy (Luke 17:11-19).[2]

- Jesus raised His friend, Lazarus, from the dead (John 11:1-44).

- Jesus prayed for His disciples (John 17:6-19).

- Jesus prayed for all believers, including you and me (John 17:20-26).

- Jesus washed His disciples' feet (John 13:2-17).

- Jesus died on the cross (Matthew 27, Mark 15, Luke 23, John 19).

The great thing is Jesus is just as active today as He was 2,000 years ago. When someone is healed from an illness through the wonders of modern science, it is because of Jesus. When someone is brought back to life by trained medical personnel, it is because of Jesus. What about those miraculous unexplained healings we often read about? It is because of Jesus. When food is placed on our meal tables, it is because of Jesus. Do you think that when Jesus prayed for all believers, including you and me, according to John 17, He stopped praying after that? No, Jesus prays for us and intercedes for us every day. His death on the cross so that our sins would be forgiven was for yesterday, today, tomorrow, and for every day thereafter until He returns. Finally, and this is what I love so much, He will still wash our feet if we simply ask Him. If we stick out our smelly, ugly, sinful feet, then our Jesus will clean them and make them new.[3] This is how Jesus served and still serves us.

So, we have been commanded to serve others regardless of their needs. We are commanded to serve as Jesus did, whether it is feeding the hungry and thirsty, clothing the naked, or anything else He leads us to do. After Jesus washed His disciples' feet, He said to wash each other's feet. I believe what Jesus is really meaning here by washing feet is to serve others and help with their needs.

Well, my friends, we have an assignment. Are we up to the task? Are we up to the mission that Jesus has placed us on? Let's do it! And do not forget to include God's Holy Spirit each time. We need His help!

Thought: When was the last time you stopped and helped another person in need?

Let us pray: Holy Spirit, guide us, lead us, direct us, and motivate us to be mindful of the needs of others. Help us to recognize a need and then go and attend to that need, all with Your help. Amen

---

[1] See Matthew 25:31-40 (NIV).

[2] This is one of my favorite healing passages. Ten were healed, but only one, of course a Samaritan, came back to give thanks to Jesus. With maybe a little wink and smile, Jesus asked, "Were not all ten cleansed? Where are the other nine?" (v. 17 NIV).

[3] I mentioned this in Day 19. I believe that Jesus washing His disciples' feet is so very important and has so much significance. It is worth repeating.

Day Twenty-Five

PATIENCE

But do not forget this one thing, dear friends: With the Lord a day is like a thousand years, and a thousand years are like a day. The Lord is not slow in keeping his promise, as some understand slowness. Instead he is patient with you, not wanting anyone to perish, but everyone to come to repentance.

—2 Peter 3:8-9 NIV

The Lord is good to those whose hope is in him, to the one who seeks him; it is good to wait quietly for the salvation of the Lord.

—Lamentations 3:25-26 NIV

I HAVE TO ADMIT, AMONG MY MANY FAULTS, I DO AT TIMES EXHIBIT AN AIR of impatience.[1] Not necessarily in everything but in some things. I will give you three examples. First is when we go to a restaurant and the hostess says the wait will be an hour.[2] I can't handle that. Second is that driver who pulls out in front of you, almost causing a wreck and then drives ten mph. Really, buddy! I thought you were late for work! Finally are those medicine packets with the plastic bubble over the pill. What were they thinking? By the time you get the pill out, the ailment has left you.[3]

Alright, enough about me. Let's talk about how our impatience operates in our lives and then how we should allow God's perfect patience to guide and direct us in all that we do.

Impatience affects how we experience life, and I am not talking about little things like the length of the wait in a restaurant. I am talking about the more important matters in our lives. We do not want to wait to find out how things are going to turn out. We want to know now. We want the results now. We want God to move quicker. We want our prayers answered sooner rather than later.

So here comes the big two questions: Do we trust God, or do we not trust God? Are we willing to wait on God's perfect timing and be patient, or are we not willing to wait? Think of a time in your life when you did not want to wait on God and decided to take the steering wheel of your life and move forward without God. How did it turn out for you? My guess is not very good. For me, it was a career move. At first, I was on my own, doing it my way, and unfortunately, the results were not positive. I realized that I needed to turn it over to God and be patient with him. Then, after a period of time, the positive results were there.

So when we start to feel that pang of impatience—that desire to try and force open that door that God has cracked open for us—we need to seek His presence, pray for guidance, and then watch how perfectly God will unfold His absolute best in His perfect timing. As the author says in our Lamentations passage, "Wait quietly." Just be at peace and sit back and relax. God has it—He really does.

Remember, my friends, we are instructed to "clothe ourselves with patience."[4]

So let's take a look at the flip side of the patience coin and talk about God's patience. God's patience simply means salvation. What do I mean by that? Look at our other passage which comes from 2 Peter. He wants everyone, yes everyone, to be saved. He does not want anyone to perish and go to hell. This patience is "immense," according to Paul in his first letter to Timothy.[5] The word "immense" is powerful—massive, colossal, and the list goes on. His patience is so huge that He is willing to wait, not push nor force on anyone acceptance of His wonderful gift of grace and salvation. He is simply willing to sit back, water some seeds that have been planted, and wait. Wait on the sinful, prideful, selfish glob called the human race because He loves us very much. He will sit there by our sides for however long it takes for us to hand over control of our lives to Him. His perfect, patient desire is for everyone to be a part of His kingdom.

So let's be patient and have faith in God, in His perfect will, and in His perfect timing. He loves us. He wants the best for us. He wants us to live with Him for all eternity. Trade in some impatience for heaven! That is quite the deal!

Thought: When was the last time you turned control of an important situation in your life over to God and you patiently waited on the outcome?

Let us pray: Dear God, when impatience creeps into our being, please assure us that You are in control and the outcome, whatever it turns out to be, will be the perfect outcome at the perfect time. Please forgive us for not trusting you as we should. We thank You for Your love and Your grace and that You truly care for us and want that relationship now and forever and ever. Amen

1 I was traumatized by our family's first family trip to Disney World in Orlando, Florida! This was before the FastPass. Therefore, you had to stand in lines for hours to get on a ride or go inside an exhibit. Imagine standing on concrete in 120-degree heat, hearing your child repeatedly say, "How much longer, Daddy?" I am certain this has been the cause of my impatience.

2 It used to be ten minutes, and my lack of patience would kick into gear. I am improving!

3 Really, you need the Jaws of Life to get that pill out!

4 See Colossians 3:12 (NIV).

5 See 1 Timothy 1:16 (NIV).

Day Twenty-Six

THE TEMPORARY LIFE

Show me, Lord, my life's end and the number of my days; let me know how fleeting my life is. You have made my days a mere handbreadth; the span of my years is as nothing before you. Everyone is but a breath, even those that seem secure.

—Psalm 39:4-5 NIV

HAVE YOU EVER FELT LIKE YOU'RE JUST LIVING THE GOOD LIFE? THAT LIFE doesn't get any better than how it is at that moment? There is certainly nothing wrong with feeling this way. Man, I have had (and currently have) a tremendous life and been blessed in so many ways. I have a wonderful family whom I love very much with Gayle, Michael, Kat, Mandy, Ford, and grand-dog Mac.[1] I have a tremendous church family at First United Methodist of Laurens and a great job. I enjoy watching the Clemson Tigers play, eating a good steak, and reading a good book in front of a fire. There are many great friends in my life, some of whom I have known for many years. What are some things you would put on your list of how great your life has been?

But while all of these things are wonderful, and God's hands are all over these blessings, we have to be careful to not allow any of them to define who we are. Why? Because they are simply a part of this life which is purely temporary. While we do not like to recognize it, admit it, or even think about it, our lives on this earth and the time we spend on this earth are just a speck of sand on the beaches of existence. In the grand scheme of things, can we compare 70, 80, or 90 years of life to all of eternity? Well, there is really no comparison, is there?

What should define you and me? What defines me is my relationship with my Lord and Savior, Jesus Christ. That is what counts. That is where the importance lies. That is where "the rubber meets the road."

But once again, I must offer another "be careful." Just because we have a relationship with Jesus does not mean the influence of this world and all of the things of this life, good or bad, will not at times take priority in our lives. I have struggled with this many times, and maybe you have too. God wants and deserves to be first in our lives and in every area of our lives. But sadly, oftentimes we put God on the shelf and replace Him with, well, with stuff.

Does God want us to have great families, meaningful jobs, or that good book to read? Absolutely! He definitely does want us to. He is the one who has provided these blessings, but He simply wants to be first on every list of our lives. Remember God is a jealous god. He loves us very much, but He never wants to be pushed to the side.

We will not take anything that we have accumulated in our life with us when we die. Why? Because so much of what we have accumulated has only temporary value and no eternal value, and there is absolutely nothing temporary that we will possess when we move our home from earth to heaven. Those nice golf clubs, that fancy car, and the important job—while nice, they are simply temporary. What has eternal value is spending time in God's word, having an active prayer life with our Creator, and showing compassion for those in need with our time, talent, and financial means.

I guess my point in this devotion is that we must stay focused and keep everything in perspective. We must never forget that this life, however great, is so temporary and our eternal home in heaven with our Creator and Savior is what counts. The psalmist in Psalm 39 says that his life (and our life) is fleeting. It passes so quickly, that dash between the date of birth and the date of death.

So one final comment and one simple thing to remember: When you are eating that steak, be sure to thank God for the steak, knowing full well that He is the one who provided that steak. Fair enough?

Thought: In what areas of your life do you need to shift focus towards things that have more eternal value?

Let us pray: Our Heavenly Creator in heaven, keep us ever so focused on You and on our eternal home that awaits us. Help us recognize that You want us to enjoy those things You have blessed us with, but help us never let our enjoyment outweigh our relationship with You. Amen.

---

[1] I guess you have noticed by now that I mention my family a considerable amount in this book. Yes, they mean a lot to me! And I know that I mean a lot to them, even with all of my "confessed imperfections" that I have made in this book!

Day Twenty-Seven

THE
EXTRAORDINARY

*God did extraordinary miracles through Paul, so that even
handkerchiefs and aprons that had touched him were taken to
the sick, and their illnesses were cured and the evil spirits left
them.*

—Acts 19:11-12 NIV

WHEN YOU SEE OR HEAR THE WORD "EXTRAORDINARY," WHAT COMES TO
mind? Maybe an extraordinary display of strength or an extraordinary act of courage. Whatever it is, it is something amazing, remark-
able, or sensational. But my favorite way to define extraordinary is
that it is something "never to be forgotten".[1]

Someone I find "never to be forgotten" is Paul. Today's passage from Acts is during one of the times Paul was traveling and preaching about the kingdom of God. He was baptizing and healing folks. As discussed in Day 19 , Paul, who was earlier known as Saul, was a hater of Christians. He hated them so much that he was instrumental in putting them in prison and even some were put to death at the hand of Saul. It all changed for Saul on that road to Damascus. God took Saul, the epitome of an enemy of God, and made him one of the most influential Christians in the history of mankind. Multiple books in the New Testament are attributed to him. Most certainly, Paul is "never to be forgotten."

So, what does this tell us? It tells us God can take you and can take me to do extraordinary things for His kingdom here on this earth. That is right! He can and will take us sinful, selfish, and, most certainly, unqualified beings and do wonders in service for Him. While it is certainly in the realm of possibility that it would be miracles of healing, I believe that it will definitely be something special even though it may appear to be small or seemingly insignificant. We need to ask our Heavenly Father to use us in whatever way He deems necessary. So I have come up with a list of some things you can do, and maybe you can relate to these.

1. On a regular basis, visit a shut-in who has no family close by.

2. Cut the grass for a neighbor who has been ill.

3. Tell five people you know who are going through difficult times that you will pray for them for a solid week.[2]

4. Prepare several full Thanksgiving meals for some absolutely needy families.

5. Take your family on a really neat and unexpected trip.

6. Always act in a manner where someone will say, "Now there goes a godly man/godly woman."

7. Drive that friend to his/her chemo treatments when the cancer has gotten to a point where they cannot drive.

8. Organize a fundraiser to help a family with their young child's medical bills.

9. Stand up for your Christian values concerning a local issue.

10. Give a Bible to someone who probably does not have one and write a personal note inside.

"Never to be forgotten" is that legacy that has a long-lasting impact. That impact will happen when we take on a particular action not for applause or recognition but for having a positive effect on a person's life.

So fill in the blank with your name. God did extraordinary things through _____. God can and will. Again, it does not have to be miracles in the traditional sense, even though it could be. It could be just those everyday acts of kindness and help. Those things that brighten someone's day. Acts of service that have meaning and purpose. It is so often said that we are here to be the hands and feet of Christ and bring honor and glory to God. This is simply the reason to be extraordinary. So let us all be extraordinary—"never to be forgotten!"

Thought: What are some ways you can be extraordinary in your life?

Let us pray: Dear God, use me to do extraordinary things for Your kingdom here on this earth. Leave a legacy of acts of help and kindness all to Your honor and glory. I am here, Lord. Use me! Amen.

[1] I am going to brag on my family some here and give examples of things they have done that are "never to be forgotten," at least by me: Michael earning the Eagle Scout Award, which is the highest achievement in scouting; Kat kicking the winning soccer goal (a tie-breaker) in the last game of her senior season but first having to shed her walking boot and crutches that she wore because of a stress fracture; Gayle, on a daily basis, taking care of Ford all day and then going to the nursing home to tend to her 94-year-old mother (LaLa and Ford are quite the team); Mandy being able to keep Michael talking for a solid four hours on their first date (I accused her of knowing more about Clemson football than he did. He was never the talker with someone he did not know.); Ford looking at me and saying, "Grandpa, I love you!"

What does the above show:

Michael: Dedication

Kat: Determination

Gayle: Loyalty (and maybe a little more energy than most her age)

Mandy: Engaging

Ford: Just the best grandson ever

[2] And actually do it. There is nothing worse than for someone to say, "You are in my thoughts and prayers," and not one prayer gets lifted up!

Day Twenty-Eight

THE PLAN

His intent was that now, through the church, the manifold wisdom of God should be made known to the rulers and authorities in the heavenly realms, according to his eternal purpose that he accomplished in Christ Jesus our Lord. In him and through faith in him we may approach God with freedom and confidence.

—Ephesians 3:10-12 NIV

THERE WAS A TELEVISION SHOW IN THE 1980S CALLED *THE A-TEAM*.[1] THE A-Team was a team of ex-special forces who set out on missions to help people fight corruption. At the conclusion of each episode, the leader of the team, Hannibal, would say, "I love it when a plan comes together."

We should always say, "I love it when God's plan always comes together." Of course, God's plan is, beginning with creation and culminating in the life and death of Jesus Christ, the most perfect plan ever devised—the redemption of the world. By no means did He haphazardly throw it together. Oh no! Certainly, we cannot make any comparisons here, but if you could, I believe God is like a brain surgeon intricately working around blood vessels, nerves, and tissue. Or like Michelangelo painting the ceiling of the Sistine Chapel in Rome with meticulous precision. How about Beethoven composing all of his masterpieces with so much clarity and purpose? God is like the surgeon, Michelangelo, and Beethoven, but so much more. God's plan is simply just perfect, filled with so much love. What makes it so much sweeter is that God's plan also includes a plan for each and every one of us.

Before any plan is implemented, there must be much thought and consideration given to its formation. What is it about? How do you achieve it? What results from the plan when it is put into place? Our passage for today references God's manifold wisdom. No question, God is very wise. But what is manifold wisdom? It is wisdom that is multi-faceted. It is multi-dimensional and all-encompassing. It is able to be applied to every situation that arises. This is wisdom at a level that our finite minds cannot even come close to comprehending. When you think of it, it would have to take this level of wisdom to accomplish all the many things that God has accomplished, and boy, has He accomplished a lot!

So let's look again at God's plan according to this passage from Ephesians. First of all, it is an eternal plan and a two-part plan. God sent His only Son, Jesus, to this earth in human form to ultimately die on the cross for the forgiveness of our sins with a wonderful eternal resurrection three days later. The second part of this plan is God establishing and cultivating a relationship with us now and for all eternity in heaven so we are able to approach God with "freedom and confidence," as Paul tells us. These two parts are inextricably tied together. While we are alive on this earth, we establish a relationship with Jesus by accepting Him as our Lord and Savior. Also, we establish a relationship with our Creator, going to Him at any time and at any place to pray, bask in His grace, accept His forgiveness, and marvel in His greatness through worship and praise. But thank goodness, things do not stop there. We believers are assured of this relationship with God and Jesus continuing for all eternity in heaven.

It is through the Church, the body of believers, that God intends to carry out His plan. That is why we are commanded to spread the Gospel message. That is why we are commanded to make disciples of all nations.

So, my friends, let's thank God every day for His plan, and once we do, then ask God's Holy Spirit to guide and direct us in whatever way to carry out His plan. Then we can say, "We love it, God, when Your plan comes together!"

Thought: Do you think God's plan also includes you? If so, in what way can you further God's plan?

Let us pray: Father God, You are so mighty and wise. It is so hard to fathom that You created this perfect plan of redemption and eternal salvation for us to have a relationship with You and Your Son, Jesus. Help me never to forget how awesome You are and how awesome Your plan is. Give me a thankful heart always for all that You do and especially for Your grace and mercy. Amen

---

[1] Have you noticed I have referenced old television shows in some of these devotionals? I like a good older television show. Of course, the best is Andy of Mayberry with the incomparable Barney Fife!

Day Twenty-Nine

GOD'S PROTECTION

The Lord your God is with you, the Mighty Warrior who saves. He will take great delight in you; in his love He will no longer rebuke you, but will rejoice over you with singing.

—Zephaniah 3:17 NIV

HOW DID YOU LEARN TO FIRST JUMP INTO A SWIMMING POOL? MAYBE you learned from a swim coach or an older sibling who pushed you into the pool and you had to doggie paddle to the side. Or was it your Mom or Dad standing there in the water with arms wide open there ready to catch you? God is there too when we find ourselves jumping into a difficult situation. He is there to catch us with arms wide open. He is there to get us through. He is there simply to take care of us. There is absolutely no problem, trial, tragedy, or situation that is too big for God. He can handle everything and anything.

Robert Jeffress, pastor, author, and news contributor, says this: "God is still on the throne, and He knows what He is doing. Relax. Trust Him. It will do wonders for your worry."[1] If we trust God, if we have absolute faith in His awesome power and ability to protect, then His protection will come through every time.

Today's passage refers to God as a "Mighty Warrior" who saves us from danger. Usually, we think of protection as keeping someone from harm. While that is true, with God, protection can mean even more than that. With God, to protect means to support, to care for, to guide and direct, and to comfort.

So, when we are facing a difficult decision to make, God will protect.

When we receive a terrible report from the doctor, God will protect,

When we are put in an unknown situation, God will protect.

When we lose a loved one to an illness or tragic accident, God will protect.

When we are passed over for that much-anticipated promotion, God will protect.

When our financial situation goes south, God will protect.

Why does God protect us? Because He loves us, and He loves us very much. According to our passage for today, God doesn't stop at just protecting us. He also rejoices with us. When we place our trust in God and He protects us in whatever situation we find ourselves in, then He rejoices with us because we have weathered the storm. We have made it through. So God says, "You trusted Me, and I protected you out of My great love for you. You have survived so it is time to celebrate. I want to rejoice with you for what you have just accomplished. It was not easy, but you made it. Come here. I want to give you a big hug! Remember, I will always catch you when you are taking that jump!"

I want to close this devotional with a quote from author Beth Moore. She says this: "We must remember we don't stand in victory because of our faith. We stand in victory because of our God. Faith in faith is pointless. Faith in a living active God moves mountains."[2]

It is our Mighty Warrior who saves. It is our Mighty Warrior who moves the mountains so we can get through that difficulty in our lives. It is our Mighty Warrior who gives us victory over every situation that we come face-to-face with. Thank you, Mighty Warrior!

Thought: When was a time God protected you?

Let us pray: Mighty Warrior God, thank You for always being there for us. Thank You for protecting us and helping us through every situation we meet. Help our faith in You to grow stronger each and every day. Amen.

---

[1] Robert Jeffress, *Invincible*. (Michigan: Baker Books, 2021), 70.

[2] McDaniel, Debbie. "30 Inspirational Beth Moore Quotes that Will Ignite Your Faith." *iBelieve*, November 7, 2016. www.ibelieve.com/faith/30-inspirational-quotes-from-beth-moore.html

Day Thirty

MAKING THE DEATH
OF JESUS PERSONAL

I have been crucified with Christ and I no longer live, but Christ lives in me. The life I now live in the body, I live by faith in the Son of God, who loved me and gave himself for me. I do not set aside the grace of God, for if righteousness could be gained through the law, Christ died for nothing.

—Galatians 2:20-21 NIV

THE CROSS IS THE BEDROCK OF THE CHRISTIAN FAITH. WITHOUT THE cross, we have nothing. I am writing this devotional a few days before Christmas, and, as we normally do, we think and talk about Jesus in the manger. In thinking about the manger and preparing for this devotional, it became abundantly clear that without the cross, there is no manger. Jesus did not have to come into this world if He did not go to the cross. The cross is the absolute key. As Paul says in today's passage, out of Jesus' great love, He died on the cross so that our sins would completely and absolutely forever be forgiven. Once we acknowledge this and truly accept Jesus as our Lord and Savior, then we are saved, and salvation is set. Through God's grace, the opportunity for us to say yes is all laid out for us on a silver platter.

I would like to share with you one of the most profound statements on salvation that I have ever come across:

> There is much more glory to God when a soul is won out of the control of Satan by means of a mere human being than if that soul had been won by direct intervention of God. God has the power to come to the world and save every individual in the flash of a second if He wished to do so. However, then Satan could well claim a sort of moral victory over God; he would have been defeated, but only by a force that was far greater than his own. But now God takes a man of the order of beings that was made lower than the angels; and in the voluntary submission of that soul to the plan of God, there is the communication of divine life.[1]

I love this statement because it gives the best explanation that I have found for the importance of there not being a wink of God's eye or a snap of His fingers providing salvation to a human being.

So why have I titled this devotion "Making the Death of Jesus Personal"? Oh, let me tell you. It is one thing to say and recognize that Christ died for the sins of the world, which He did. But it is another to say that Christ died for *me.* Paul recognized this in this passage from Galatians. When we believers fully appreciate that Christ's death was for us individually, then our relationship becomes more personal, more real, and more satisfying. It takes joy to the next level.

But let's look at the flip side of our personal coin. Look at the two words above–"voluntary submission." We play a huge part in our salvation. By God's amazing grace, he offers us forgiveness and salvation through Christ's death on the cross, but it is up to us to accept it or not. Sadly, many people do not. But our playing a part makes it so much more personal. When we play a role in something great and fantastic, isn't there more meaning and value? For example, imagine your team wins the championship. That is great and wonderful. But if you played a vital role in that winning touchdown, doesn't the meaning and value of that championship win just increase? Then we add "icing to the cake" to get to see the look on the face of a defeated Satan when one's heart is turned over to Jesus. It's another death blow to Satan in the battle with the evil one. Yes, Satan is once again defeated by a mere human being who Satan cares nothing about but whom God loves immensely.

We always need to make the death of Jesus personal. We make it personal in our relationship with Him who took on the sins of you and of me in voluntarily dying that horrible death on the cross. We make it personal in our relationship with God by fully accepting and appreciating that free unmerited favor of God which we call grace. Relationships must always be personal. Make yours personal today.

Thought: Have you ever given it any thought to this truth that the cross is so personal? How do you make the cross personal for you?

Let us pray: Precious Jesus, You died for me two thousand years ago on that cross. You did it for me so that my sins would be forgiven and so that I could stand before our Heavenly Father and receive eternal salvation. Jesus, You did this for me, and I am so very thankful. Amen.

[1] Donald Grey Barnhouse, *Romans, Chapters 1.1-5.1.* (Hendrickson Publishers Marketing, LLC, 1959), 186.

Day Thirty-One

GOD'S LOVE

*For I am convinced that neither death nor life, neither angels
nor demons, neither the present nor the future, nor any powers, neither height nor depth, nor anything else in all creation,
will be able to separate us from the love of God that is in Christ
Jesus our Lord.*

—Romans 8:38-39

ONE THING THAT NEVER CHANGES IS THAT GOD IS LOVE AND HE LOVES
us very much. We know with absolute certainty that God loves us
unconditionally. Let's try and put this in perspective. Those of us
who have children can honestly say, without exception, that we love
our children unconditionally. Have we liked some of the things they
did growing up?[1] No, we did not. But did it alter the love that we
had for them? No, it did not.

God is the same way but on a much higher level than we can ever imagine. There is nothing we can do to change or lessen God's love for us. There is nothing in this entire universe that will cause our Heavenly Father to love us any less. Even the ultimate demon himself, Satan, cannot do anything to us that will cause God to think twice about His love for us.

I think about the most recognized and most-quoted passage of scripture found in the Gospel of John which reads, "For God so loved the world that he gave his one and only son, that whoever believes in him shall not perish but have eternal life."[2] He did this for everyone because God loves everyone. God allowed His Son, Jesus, to die that horrible death on the cross for you and for me so that our sins would forever be forgiven.

I am reminded of a story I heard several years ago. When a man was growing up, his mom sometimes liked to cook breakfast food at supper time. She had worked a full day on her job, and when she got home, she was very tired. Nonetheless, she prepared the breakfast meal for supper, but she burned the biscuits. When she put the plate, including the biscuits, in front of this man's dad, the dad, without missing a beat, started putting butter and jelly on a burnt biscuit and took a couple of good bites. Later, this man could overhear his mom apologize to the dad for burning the biscuits, and the dad replied, "Don't worry honey. I like burnt biscuits."

When it was time for bed, the man went to his father and asked, "Dad, do you really like burnt biscuits?"

The dad responded, "Son, Mom was really tired tonight, and really, burnt biscuits won't hurt anyone."

The moral of the story is this: We all make mistakes. We all have imperfections. We should always accept everyone even with their flaws.

God does this. He accepts us as we are with our many imperfections. He loves us exactly as we are in spite of our sinful nature. Paul also tells us that "God demonstrates his own love for us in this: While we were still sinners, Christ died for us."[3] This is so amazing!

God hates sin so much that He allowed His Son to die, but He did so because of His love for us—His unconditional love for us!

So when we tell that little (or big) lie, remember God still loves us.

When we place an idol in our lives ahead of God, remember God still loves us.

When we are deceitful and dishonest, remember God still loves us.

When we show hate to our fellow neighbor, remember God still loves us.

When we fail to show mercy to a person in need, remember God still loves us.

When we allow our pride to overshadow our humility, remember God still loves us.

When we are envious and covet what another has, remember God still loves us.

When we are greedy and fail to share with others, remember God still loves us.

But I will state this. We should not and cannot allow ourselves to falsely believe God's unconditional love for us is in some way a license to sin. It is not. God still expects us to confess and repent of our sins. Even though His unconditional love will never change, He is still a God of justice, and when He believes punishment of some sort is necessary, I can assure you that is exactly what will happen. God expects all of us to strive towards perfection to be more Christ-like in our character and actions. God's love actually causes us to want to act more like Christ and not do bad things anymore. But, when we get out of line, there will be consequences. We just always need to remember this.

Again, remember that God will always love us and that will never ever change. Hallelujah! Thank you, Lord!

Thought: How do you experience God's love on a daily basis?

Let us pray: Dear heavenly, loving, and gracious God, You are such a loving God. You love us so much that You gave Your most precious Son to die for us. We are so sinful, yet You did this for us. We are so eternally thankful for Your love. We love You, too! Amen and amen.

---

[1] Hey, Michael and Kat! I was going to put some of your teenage mishaps in this devotional. Naw, I decided not to, but it was tempting!

[2] John 3:16 NIV. Also mentioned in Day Three.

[3] Romans 5:8 NIV

Conclusion

A PRAYER FROM JESUS

My prayer is not for them alone. I pray also for those who will believe in me through their message, that all of them may be one, Father, just as you are in me and I am in you. May they also be in us so that the world may believe that you have sent me. I have given them the glory that you gave me, that they may be one as we are one—I in them and you in me—so that they may be brought to complete unity. Then the world will know that you sent me and have loved them even as you have loved me. Father, I want those you have given me to be with me where I am, and to see my glory, the glory you have given me because you loved me before the creation of the world. Righteous Father, though the world does not know you, I know you, and they know that you have sent me. I have made you known to them, and will continue to make you known in order that the love you have for me may be in them and that I myself may be in them.

—John 17:20-26 NIV

JESUS IS THE ULTIMATE PRAYER WARRIOR! JESUS CONCLUDED HIS TIME with His disciples before His arrest and death on the cross by praying to be glorified, by praying for His disciples, and then praying for you and for me. Yes, for you and for me. Praying for all believers now and yet to come. Is that not just wonderful?

I hope you have noticed that I have talked a lot about Jesus and the cross. Without question, it is so absolutely necessary in our Christian walk and faith to have that constant reminder and recognition that Jesus died for us. Nothing more, and nothing less!

I just hope that you find Jesus' prayer in the Gospel of John to be a fitting conclusion to this devotional book. And to my beloved dachshund, Lucy, see you in heaven one day!

Made in the USA
Columbia, SC
03 September 2023

22340957R00086